DO Drops
Volume 6

DO Drops

Volume 6

Daily Bible Devotional

Dr. Bo Wagner

Word of His Mouth Publishers
Mooresboro, NC

All Scripture quotations are taken from the **King James Version** of the Bible.

ISBN: 978-1-941039-29-8
Printed in the United States of America
©2021 Dr. Bo Wagner (Robert Arthur Wagner)

Word of His Mouth Publishers
Mooresboro, NC
www.wordofhismouth.com

Cover art by Chip Nuhrah

Devotion 1

King Ahaziah worshiped Baal. Not in name only; he was a true devotee. Notice what he did in his hour of desperation:

2 Kings 1:1 *Then Moab rebelled against Israel after the death of Ahab.* **2** *And Ahaziah fell down through a lattice in his upper chamber that was in Samaria, and was sick: and he sent messengers, and said unto them, Go, enquire of Baalzebub the god of Ekron whether I shall recover of this disease.*

Injured, diseased because of that injury, Ahaziah rightly feared death. And so he reached out to his "god" via messengers. But did you notice what that reaching out consisted of? Ahaziah asked the messengers to go ask Baal if he would die, but he did not get them to ask Baal to heal him! There is a simple reason for that—Baal never healed anyone. In fact, Baal never actually did anything for anyone. The extent of his "power" was supposedly having his "prophets" tell people what was or was not going to happen.

To quote the Hulk, "Puny god."

DO praise and worship the true God. Not only can He answer your concerns, but He can also alter your circumstances!

Personal Notes:

_____
_____
_____
_____
_____
_____
_____
_____
_____
_____
_____
_____
_____
_____
_____
_____
_____
_____
_____
_____
_____
_____
_____
_____
_____
_____
_____
_____

Devotion 2

Ahaziah was clearly expecting his messengers to be gone for a while. But something happened along the way.

2 Kings 1:3 *But the angel of the LORD said to Elijah the Tishbite, Arise, go up to meet the messengers of the king of Samaria, and say unto them, Is it not because there is not a God in Israel, that ye go to enquire of Baalzebub the god of Ekron?* **4** *Now therefore thus saith the LORD, Thou shalt not come down from that bed on which thou art gone up, but shalt surely die. And Elijah departed.* **5** *And when the messengers turned back unto him, he said unto them, Why are ye now turned back?* **6** *And they said unto him, There came a man up to meet us, and said unto us, Go, turn again unto the king that sent you, and say unto him, Thus saith the LORD, Is it not because there is not a God in Israel, that thou sendest to enquire of Baalzebub the god of Ekron? therefore thou shalt not come down from that bed on which thou art gone up, but shalt surely die.*

When David was facing Goliath, he was able to say, "*There is a God in Israel!*" But after years of wicked king after wicked king, Elijah said, "*There is not a God in Israel.*"

Had God ceased to be omnipresent? Certainly not. But He had ceased to "be in Israel" in the sense of making Himself clearly known and having communion with His people. Their sin had made Him withdraw from them, and all they were left with was the pathetic, powerless, false god of the Philistines.

8

DO prize the presence of God so much that you would never do anything to push Him away!

Personal Notes:

_____

_____

_____

_____

_____

_____

_____

_____

_____

_____

_____

_____

_____

_____

_____

_____

_____

_____

_____

_____

_____

_____

_____

_____

_____

Devotion 3

The messengers had returned to king Ahaziah with a message that some prophet had intercepted them and told them that the king would die. But do you know what they apparently did not even think to ask this stranger?

Who he was!

So, the king had to try and figure it out. And figure it out he did:

2 Kings 1:7 *And he said unto them, What manner of man was he which came up to meet you, and told you these words?* **8** *And they answered him, He was an hairy man, and girt with a girdle of leather about his loins. And he said, It is Elijah the Tishbite.*

I find it fascinating that the king knew that it was Elijah just by a description of his appearance. In short, Elijah had a simple, rough, masculine appearance about him. His clothes were plain and rough, and he was hairy, most likely meaning that he had the long beard so commonly worn by the prophets.

Even the appearance of a child of God ought to be distinct. Especially for men, in this world that uses terms like "toxic masculinity" to try and make men nothing but bigger versions of women, people ought to be able to tell who we are and what we are.

Christian ladies, DO be ladies, and Christian men, DO be men!

Personal Notes:

Devotion 4

Wicked king Ahaziah had sent his messengers to Baal to find out if he would live, but they had been intercepted by Elijah and come right back to the king. They had delivered Elijah's blunt message; Ahaziah was going to die.

Now, it seems at a time like that, and knowing the reputation of Elijah, the king would have been humble and sought after Elijah for mercy and help. That, alas, is not the route he chose. He sent a company of the army out after Elijah.

2 Kings 1:9 *Then the king sent unto him a captain of fifty with his fifty. And he went up to him: and, behold, he sat on the top of an hill. And he spake unto him, Thou man of God, the king hath said, Come down.*

Fifty-one aggressive men, with a haughty, forceful message, that went something along the lines of, "Hey, preacher man, the king demands that you present yourself to him!" That was not going to work out so well:

2 Kings 1:10 *And Elijah answered and said to the captain of fifty, If I be a man of God, then let fire come down from heaven, and consume thee and thy fifty. And there came down fire from heaven, and consumed him and his fifty.*

Fifty-one men died for one reason: the king was a haughty, heedless jerk. His mouth and attitude cost the lives of fifty-one men—husbands, fathers, brothers, sons.

DO remember that your attitude will not just bring you blessing or blistering; it will also bring either collateral delight or collateral damage!

Personal Notes:

_____

_____

_____

_____

_____

_____

_____

_____

_____

_____

_____

_____

_____

_____

_____

_____

_____

_____

_____

_____

_____

_____

_____

_____

Devotion 5

After fire fell from heaven and consumed fifty-one men, someone told the king what had happened and that Elijah was still not budging from the top of the hill. So, what did king "I-don't-care-about-anyone-but-me" do next?

2 Kings 1:11 *Again also he sent unto him another captain of fifty with his fifty. And he answered and said unto him, O man of God, thus hath the king said, Come down quickly.*

At this point, I do not know at whom I am more bewildered; the king, who obviously did not care that he was putting lives at risk, or the second captain, who marched his fifty men across the charred, smoking bones of the previous fifty-one men in order to do the exact same thing and expect different results!

The results were not different. At all.

2 Kings 1:12 *And Elijah answered and said unto them, If I be a man of God, let fire come down from heaven, and consume thee and thy fifty. And the fire of God came down from heaven, and consumed him and his fifty.*

Now there were one hundred and two piles of smoking bones on the hillside.

If a person cannot learn from the mistakes of others, he or she does not need to be leading anyone in anything!

DO make a habit of learning from the mistakes of others. It is a "bare-bones" way of making sure you do not end up "smoking hot" in the absolute worst kind of way!

Personal Notes:

_____

_____

_____

_____

_____

_____

_____

_____

_____

_____

_____

_____

_____

_____

_____

_____

_____

_____

_____

_____

_____

_____

_____

_____

_____

_____

_____

Devotion 6

After Company B marched up the hill and joined Company A in the "Instant Charcoal Briquette Hall of Fame," the king, bless his single-digit IQ, sent yet a third company up the hill after Elijah. Fortunately, this company was led by a man with both character and intelligence.

2 Kings 1:13 *And he sent again a captain of the third fifty with his fifty. And the third captain of fifty went up, and came and fell on his knees before Elijah, and besought him, and said unto him, O man of God, I pray thee, let my life, and the life of these fifty thy servants, be precious in thy sight.* **14** *Behold, there came fire down from heaven, and burnt up the two captains of the former fifties with their fifties: therefore let my life now be precious in thy sight.* **15** *And the angel of the LORD said unto Elijah, Go down with him: be not afraid of him. And he arose, and went down with him unto the king.*

This captain disobeyed his king. He did not give the message he was ordered to give. And in that "rebellion," he saved the lives of fifty innocent men. So, is it always wrong to defy and disobey orders and authority? If you say yes, congratulations. Not only have you condemned this captain for saving fifty lives, but you have also placed your stamp of approval on the slaughter of six million Jews in Nazi Germany.

DO understand that your highest responsibility is to obey God, and sometimes that will require you to disobey man!

Personal Notes:

_____
_____
_____
_____
_____
_____
_____
_____
_____
_____
_____
_____
_____
_____
_____
_____
_____
_____
_____
_____
_____
_____
_____
_____
_____
_____
_____
_____

Devotion 7

Once Elijah came down from the hill with the third captain, he came to King Ahaziah, who, by the way, simply could have asked nicely the first time and avoided the loss of one hundred and two innocent men. When Elijah walked in and stood before the king, he delivered the same message he had already sent.

2 Kings 1:16 *And he said unto him, Thus saith the LORD, Forasmuch as thou hast sent messengers to enquire of Baalzebub the god of Ekron, is it not because there is no God in Israel to enquire of his word? therefore thou shalt not come down off that bed on which thou art gone up, but shalt surely die.* **17** *So he died according to the word of the LORD which Elijah had spoken. And Jehoram reigned in his stead in the second year of Jehoram the son of Jehoshaphat king of Judah; because he had no son.*

Ahaziah would die of his sickness specifically because he worshiped Baal and sent to Baal when he needed "god's help."

In other words, God was not going to kill Ahaziah; He was simply going to let Ahaziah's "god" be responsible for healing him. And since Ahaziah's god could not do that, he was going to die.

Trust the wrong god, get the wrong results.

DO be sure you are trusting the right God! May I recommend the One who created life, gave His life, and raised Himself back to life after He had been dead for three days? Since He is the real God, DO trust Him!

18

Personal Notes:

_____
_____
_____
_____
_____
_____
_____
_____
_____
_____
_____
_____
_____
_____
_____
_____
_____
_____
_____
_____
_____
_____
_____
_____
_____
_____
_____
_____

Devotion 8

The life of the great Elijah was coming to a close. But what amazes me is how calmly and casually the Bible describes the utterly unorthodox way it was going to come to an end.

2 Kings 2:1 *And it came to pass, when the LORD would take up Elijah into heaven by a whirlwind, that Elijah went with Elisha from Gilgal.*

There are times when I want to look at the words of Scripture and say, "Wait, what?" What, again, did the text say about the end of Elijah? "*It came to pass, when the LORD would take up Elijah into heaven by a whirlwind...*"

That had never been done before in the history of humanity. From the Garden of Eden up until then, every single human being whose life on earth had ended had done so by way of death, save for Enoch, who "walked with God and was not, for God took him." Elijah was about to leave this life and go into eternity via a brand spanking new way; a whirlwind was going to pick him up and physically carry him into heaven!

If God chose to take us into heaven by putting us in an envelope and mailing us there, it would work.

DO recognize that, while God often does the same thing the same way over and over again, He is so much God that, at the drop of a hat, He can do some normal thing in such a unique way that it could only be Him!

Personal Notes:

Devotion 9

Elijah was getting ready to leave for heaven. And he tried very hard to separate himself from Elisha before that happened. Elisha, though, could not be dissuaded from following after him.

2 Kings 2:2 *And Elijah said unto Elisha, Tarry here, I pray thee; for the LORD hath sent me to Bethel. And Elisha said unto him, As the LORD liveth, and as thy soul liveth, I will not leave thee. So they went down to Bethel.* **3** *And the sons of the prophets that were at Bethel came forth to Elisha, and said unto him, Knowest thou that the LORD will take away thy master from thy head to day? And he said, Yea, I know it; hold ye your peace.* **4** *And Elijah said unto him, Elisha, tarry here, I pray thee; for the LORD hath sent me to Jericho. And he said, As the LORD liveth, and as thy soul liveth, I will not leave thee. So they came to Jericho.* **5** *And the sons of the prophets that were at Jericho came to Elisha, and said unto him, Knowest thou that the LORD will take away thy master from thy head to day? And he answered, Yea, I know it; hold ye your peace.* **6** *And Elijah said unto him, Tarry, I pray thee, here; for the LORD hath sent me to Jordan. And he said, As the LORD liveth, and as thy soul liveth, I will not leave thee. And they two went on.*

From Gilgal to Bethel was about fifteen miles. From Bethel to Jericho was another twelve. From Jericho to the Jordan was another five or so. Elisha trekked or rode with him step-for-step for thirty-two miles or more, just to be there at the end.

That is faithfulness and friendship.

DO be able to be counted on like that! For everything great that Elisha ever did, this, to Elijah, was likely the greatest of all!

Personal Notes:

_____

_____

_____

_____

_____

_____

_____

_____

_____

_____

_____

_____

_____

_____

_____

_____

_____

_____

_____

_____

_____

_____

_____

_____

_____

_____

_____

Devotion 10

Elijah and Elisha were nearing the end of their journey together. Elijah was about to be taken to heaven by a whirlwind, and Elisha was sticking with him every step of the way. But in between them and the "launch point," if you will, was the Jordan River. Somehow, they would have to get across that.

And Elijah was ready.

2 Kings 2:8 *And Elijah took his mantle, and wrapped it together, and smote the waters, and they were divided hither and thither, so that they two went over on dry ground.*

The first five times the phrase "dry ground" is used in Scripture, it refers to water being miraculously parted so that someone could get to the other side. The first time is the most famous, the parting of the Red Sea itself so that an entire nation could cross over. The second time was almost that impressive, where this very Jordan River was parted so that, once again, the whole nation could pass over.

But this third occurrence is not nearly as well know or as often spoken of. In this instance, the Jordan River has parted once again. This time this astonishing miracle took place for the benefit of just two people, Elijah and Elisha. God demonstrated that He is not just concerned with the masses and multitudes but also with the needs of individuals. God is just as willing to come through for one or two as He is for one or two million!

DO be willing to trust God to "be as big" for you as He is for nations and kingdoms!

Personal Notes:

_____
_____
_____
_____
_____
_____
_____
_____
_____
_____
_____
_____
_____
_____
_____
_____
_____
_____
_____
_____
_____
_____
_____
_____
_____
_____
_____
_____
_____
_____

Devotion 11

Once Elijah and Elisha were over the Jordan, Elijah turned his attention to this faithful friend who would be stepping into his shoes before the day was done. He wanted to give Elisha something before he left.

2 Kings 2:9 *And it came to pass, when they were gone over, that Elijah said unto Elisha, Ask what I shall do for thee, before I be taken away from thee. And Elisha said, I pray thee, let a double portion of thy spirit be upon me.*

Many people, when asked what they want, come back with the standard answer:

"Whatever. Anything is fine."

Not Elisha. Elisha "asked big." He did not want money or fame or land; he wanted a double portion of the spirit of Elijah. To put it in practical terms, he wanted to be twice the preacher, twice the prophet, and twice the miracle worker that Elijah had been.

All of this had to be the work of God; man could never give such a gift. Nonetheless, Elijah clearly had assurance from heaven that the request would be met, but under one condition:

2 Kings 2:10 *And he said, Thou hast asked a hard thing: nevertheless, if thou see me when I am taken from thee, it shall be so unto thee; but if not, it shall not be so.*

Is that an odd requirement for the request to be met? Not really. Let me paraphrase it this way: "If you keep your eye on the prize until the very end, if you do not waver a bit or allow yourself to get distracted, you will get God's best for you."

And that is pretty much the way it always works. So DO be faithful and undistracted in your walk with the Lord!

Personal Notes:

_____

_____

_____

_____

_____

_____

_____

_____

_____

_____

_____

_____

_____

_____

_____

_____

_____

_____

_____

_____

_____

_____

_____

_____

_____

_____

_____

Devotion 12

Elijah and Elisha continued to walk and talk. It is fairly evident from the text that the whirlwind that would carry Elijah into heaven was an expected thing. No doubt they were both watching for that, looking at the clouds, glancing to the sky.

But then came something that was clearly unexpected:

2 Kings 2:11 *And it came to pass, as they still went on, and talked, that, behold, there appeared a chariot of fire, and horses of fire, and parted them both asunder; and Elijah went up by a whirlwind into heaven.*

Lest you misunderstand, God did not "create something new" for Elijah. Elisha would later on see that with his own eyes:

2 Kings 6:17 *And Elisha prayed, and said, LORD, I pray thee, open his eyes, that he may see. And the LORD opened the eyes of the young man; and he saw: and, behold, the mountain was full of horses and chariots of fire round about Elisha.*

There is an unseen, spiritual world all around us. God made part of that world visible to Elijah and Elisha in the very last seconds of Elijah's earthly life. But that unseen world, those angels and chariots of fire, had been there the entire time!

DO understand that while the physical world is a gift from God, it is also only the tip of the unseen iceberg!

Personal Notes:

_____

_____

_____

_____

_____

_____

_____

_____

_____

_____

_____

_____

_____

_____

_____

_____

_____

_____

_____

_____

_____

_____

_____

_____

_____

_____

_____

_____

Devotion 13

As Elijah was taken from him, Elisha cried out in recognition of what was happening:

2 Kings 2:12 *And Elisha saw it, and he cried, My father, my father, the chariot of Israel, and the horsemen thereof. And he saw him no more: and he took hold of his own clothes, and rent them in two pieces.*

Elijah had told Elisha that he must see him the very moment he was taken, or he would not receive what he had asked for, a double portion of the spirit of Elijah. Elisha, ever watchful, did see. And the last words Elijah heard him speak as he was taken up from him were "My father, my father, the chariot of Israel, and the horsemen thereof."

The way that Elisha referred to Elijah, as "*my father, my father,*" was a powerful tribute to the influential role Elijah had played in his life. The cry of, "*the chariot of Israel, and the horsemen thereof*" was a testimony that he knew that God was the one now taking Elijah away. In other words, Elisha at that moment spoke words of tribute to Elijah and words of deference to God. Elisha did not like losing Elijah, but he was willing to let God be God even in this.

DO be willing to give honor to whom it is due, and DO also be willing to give God the humble respect and submission that He deserves, even in things we wish did not have to be!

Personal Notes:

_____
_____
_____
_____
_____
_____
_____
_____
_____
_____
_____
_____
_____
_____
_____
_____
_____
_____
_____
_____
_____
_____
_____
_____
_____
_____
_____
_____

Devotion 14

Elijah was gone, and, whether Elisha knew it yet or not, a double portion of Elijah's spirit now lay on him. He had asked for it. Now he was going to pick up the mantle of Elijah and put it to the test.

2 Kings 2:13 *He took up also the mantle of Elijah that fell from him, and went back, and stood by the bank of Jordan;* **14** *And he took the mantle of Elijah that fell from him, and smote the waters, and said, Where is the LORD God of Elijah? and when he also had smitten the waters, they parted hither and thither: and Elisha went over.*

The question of Elisha spoke volumes about his understanding of the situation. Did he want the power of Elijah? Yes. Had it been given to him? Yes. But where did that power come from? Elisha knew that it did not come from Elijah. As he smote the waters he did not ask, "Where is Elijah?" he asked, *"Where is the LORD God of Elijah?"*

And God answered the question for him. The waters of the Jordan, which just minutes earlier had been parted by Elijah for two to pass over, now were parted again for just one to pass back over. The "parting waters for a nation" God, which he learned was also the "parting waters for a duo" God, was also, to his delight, the "parting the waters for one" God.

We so often think of spiritual giants of the past and ask, "Where have all the old warhorses gone?" What we should be asking is, "Where is the God of the old warhorses?"

DO remember that our power does not come from the great leaders of the past; our power comes from the God who is always present!

Personal Notes:

_____
_____
_____
_____
_____
_____
_____
_____
_____
_____
_____
_____
_____
_____
_____
_____
_____
_____
_____
_____
_____
_____
_____
_____
_____
_____

Devotion 15

Both Elijah and the Jordan were now behind him. Elisha was now moving forward to do the work that God had called him to do. But unfortunately, some very well-meaning people could not quite let go just yet.

2 Kings 2:15 *And when the sons of the prophets which were to view at Jericho saw him, they said, The spirit of Elijah doth rest on Elisha. And they came to meet him, and bowed themselves to the ground before him.* **16** *And they said unto him, Behold now, there be with thy servants fifty strong men; let them go, we pray thee, and seek thy master: lest peradventure the Spirit of the LORD hath taken him up, and cast him upon some mountain, or into some valley. And he said, Ye shall not send.* **17** *And when they urged him till he was ashamed, he said, Send. They sent therefore fifty men; and they sought three days, but found him not.* **18** *And when they came again to him, (for he tarried at Jericho,) he said unto them, Did I not say unto you, Go not?*

This is one of the clearest examples in the Bible of an "I told you so!" After wasting three days searching for a man that Elisha knew was already in heaven, Elisha told them, "*Did I not say unto you, Go not?*"

Good intentions and good ideas are often two very different things.

In this case, it was only three days of time and effort that were wasted. In some cases, the cost is far more significant. The distinguishing difference between good ideas and good intentions usually comes down to this question, "Is it what God wants?" The serpent convinced Eve that he had good intentions for the lie he was selling her. But her tipoff that it was a bad idea should have been the fact that she knew God did not want it!

DO have enough spiritual discernment to distinguish between good intentions and actual good ideas!

Personal Notes:

_____

_____

_____

_____

_____

_____

_____

_____

_____

_____

_____

_____

_____

_____

_____

_____

_____

_____

_____

_____

_____

_____

Devotion 16

Elisha was at Jericho and had just given his "I told you so" to the well-meaning men who spent three days searching for Elijah. Now, though, everyone needed to pick up with life and carry on. Thus it is that we find the men of the city speaking to Elisha about the living situation there in Jericho.

2 Kings 2:19 *And the men of the city said unto Elisha, Behold, I pray thee, the situation of this city is pleasant, as my lord seeth: but the water is naught, and the ground barren.*

Jericho was a city in a lovely location with a lethal problem. Somehow the waters had become bitter, and they were so bad that the land itself was dying, nothing would grow. It had not always been like that, or no one would ever have built there to begin with. Jericho had been destroyed by Joshua and the Israelites hundreds of years earlier during the conquest of Canaan. God had commanded it never to be rebuilt, then had prophesied that a disobedient man would rebuild it, and it would cost him the lives of both of his sons. And that is exactly what happened when Hiel the Bethelite rebuilt it.

So, Jericho had a legacy of sin and rebellion. And yet God did not hold the past actions of others against the current inhabitants. When they needed help, God used Elisha and gave that help:

2 Kings 2:20 *And he said, Bring me a new cruse, and put salt therein. And they brought it to him.* **21** *And he went forth unto the spring of the waters, and cast the salt in there, and said, Thus saith the*

LORD, I have healed these waters; there shall not be from thence any more death or barren land. **22** *So the waters were healed unto this day, according to the saying of Elisha which he spake.*

DO know that God never looks at your parents or grandparents when deciding how He views you!

Personal Notes:

_____

_____

_____

_____

_____

_____

_____

_____

_____

_____

_____

_____

_____

_____

_____

_____

_____

_____

_____

_____

_____

_____

_____

_____

Devotion 17

Jericho and Bethel, while not too far apart geographically, were light years apart in how they thought of God and His man. When Elisha left Jericho and went to Bethel, he received a very cutting welcome.

2 Kings 2:23 *And he went up from thence unto Bethel: and as he was going up by the way, there came forth little children out of the city, and mocked him, and said unto him, Go up, thou bald head; go up, thou bald head.* **24** *And he turned back, and looked on them, and cursed them in the name of the LORD. And there came forth two she bears out of the wood, and tare forty and two children of them.*

This is one of the most shocking passages in the Bible, and also one of the most misunderstood. We will look at this passage for a couple of days before we move on, to make sure you understand and apply it correctly.

To begin with, notice the taunt of "go up" that was hurled at Elisha. That should be familiar to you. Elijah had just gone up into heaven, and everyone knew it. When "thou bald head" was added, it was an extra measure of insult. That was a euphemism in their day for "numbskull, empty head," or as people today would say, "idiot." They were saying "We didn't like Elijah; we don't like you; you are an idiot; why don't you just ride on up to heaven and be gone too!"

These words were spoken to Elisha during his darkest days, days of mourning, when he was missing

38

the one who had meant the most to him. This was a "theological taunt;" not some mere babbling of toddlers. These "children" were old enough to be outside the city without parents and to "intelligently taunt" Elisha.

DO understand that children are capable of great wickedness much earlier than they are usually given credit for! Wise parents will realize that and will put away the rose-colored glasses when viewing their kids!

Personal Notes:

_____
_____
_____
_____
_____
_____
_____
_____
_____
_____
_____
_____
_____
_____
_____
_____
_____
_____
_____
_____
_____

Devotion 18

We began yesterday looking at the confrontation between Elisha and the youth of Bethel. They instigated a confrontation with him, and basically called him an empty-headed idiot, and told him to go on up to heaven as Elijah did. Here once again is that attack and the response.

2 Kings 2:23 *And he went up from thence unto Bethel: and as he was going up by the way, there came forth little children out of the city, and mocked him, and said unto him, Go up, thou bald head; go up, thou bald head.* **24** *And he turned back, and looked on them, and cursed them in the name of the LORD. And there came forth two she bears out of the wood, and tare forty and two children of them.*

It is easy to see why scoffers and atheists love this passage. This seeming "overreaction" to "innocent kids teasing a man" is used day in and day out to paint God and Elisha in a bad light.

But do you notice a key difference between the two verses? Verse twenty-three says "*little children*" came out to mock. But verse twenty-four says the bears tare forty-two "*children of them.*" The word "little" is gone in that verse, and rightly so. The word "children" in those two verses is also from two different words! In other words, a huge group of "children," some younger and some much older, came out to attack Elisha. But when God sent the two bears rolling through to defend His man, only the older ones were even attacked. And even then, while people always use the word "killed," the Bible does

40

not! It simply uses the word "tare," or as we would say, "tore."

So, God carefully sent those bears after the older instigators, sparing the "little children," and dealing with the older ones (who, based on the word used for them, would be in our day classified as young adults) in perfect measure.

DO realize that everything God does, He does perfectly, even the things that at first blush make us gasp!

Personal Notes:

_____

_____

_____

_____

_____

_____

_____

_____

_____

_____

_____

_____

_____

_____

_____

_____

_____

_____

_____

_____

Devotion 19

As 2 Kings 3 begins, the scene shifts back to political issues. Jehoram, son of the late Ahab, is on the throne of Israel, the Northern Kingdom. Jehoshaphat, who had once unwisely linked himself with Jehoram's father, Ahab, is still on the throne of Judah, the Southern Kingdom.

Moab, who was under tribute to Ahab, has now rebelled against his son, Jehoram. So Jehoram did as his father had done and called Jehoshaphat to come with him to battle against them. The last time something like this happened, Jehoshaphat nearly lost his life.

So how will he respond this time?

2 Kings 3:7 *And he went and sent to Jehoshaphat the king of Judah, saying, The king of Moab hath rebelled against me: wilt thou go with me against Moab to battle? And he said, I will go up: I am as thou art, my people as thy people, and my horses as thy horses.*

That should sound familiar to you. Here is what he said some years before that time when Ahab nearly got him killed:

1 Kings 22:4 *And he said unto Jehoshaphat, Wilt thou go with me to battle to Ramothgilead? And Jehoshaphat said to the king of Israel, I am as thou art, my people as thy people, my horses as thy horses.*

It is like listening to a recording! Jehoshaphat was one of those frustrating people who just never learn. If you slammed him on the left foot with a sledgehammer, he would let you do the same thing to the right foot, figuring that the result may be different.

DO learn, and every day change for the better based on that learning!

Personal Notes:

_____

_____

_____

_____

_____

_____

_____

_____

_____

_____

_____

_____

_____

_____

_____

_____

_____

_____

_____

_____

_____

_____

_____

_____

_____

_____

_____

Devotion 20

Jehoshaphat had once again been dumb enough to link up with a wicked king of the house of Ahab. And, again, it was very nearly a fatal choice.

2 Kings 3:8 *And he said, Which way shall we go up? And he answered, The way through the wilderness of Edom.* **9** *So the king of Israel went, and the king of Judah, and the king of Edom: and they fetched a compass of seven days' journey: and there was no water for the host, and for the cattle that followed them.* **10** *And the king of Israel said, Alas! that the LORD hath called these three kings together, to deliver them into the hand of Moab!*

The first time Jehoshaphat nearly died in battle. This time he, and many others, were about to die of thirst. The king of Israel led them into a barren wilderness with no water... and then whined something like, "Why, oh why has God done this to us!"

If we were playing "pin the tail on the donkey," either king would be a winner; Jehoram for being such a poor leader, or Jehoshaphat for once again being willing to follow the house of Ahab.

DO choose your "leaders" carefully!

Personal Notes:

Devotion 21

Once again Jehoshaphat was in trouble due to joining up with the house of Ahab. That is the bad news. The good news is that he had the sense, once again, to call for a real man of God to ask for advice. Mind you, the last time he did so, he and everyone else simply ignored that advice, but that is another issue altogether. Here is how things began this time around:

2 Kings 3:11 *But Jehoshaphat said, Is there not here a prophet of the LORD, that we may enquire of the LORD by him? And one of the king of Israel's servants answered and said, Here is Elisha the son of Shaphat, which poured water on the hands of Elijah.* **12** *And Jehoshaphat said, The word of the LORD is with him. So the king of Israel and Jehoshaphat and the king of Edom went down to him.*

Jehoshaphat asked for a prophet of the LORD. Amazingly, it was one of the king of Israel's servants who knew just who to turn to. He told them that Elisha was nearby. But it is the way that he described him that is so incredible: "Here is Elisha the son of Shaphat, which poured water on the hands of Elijah."

When people think of ministry, they usually thinking of leading and being followed. But Elisha, now the main prophet in Israel, was where he was because of the years he spent "pouring water on the hands of Elijah." He made himself Elijah's servant; he tended to his needs; he followed him around and did whatever he needed to have done.

Little wonder, then, that he received a double portion of Elijah's spirit and ended up doing twice the number of miracles that Elijah himself did. The God who later wrapped Himself in a towel and washed the dirty feet of His disciples prizes a servant's heart and picks those who have such a heart for His greatest tasks!

DO be willing to be a "water pourer" if you ever expect to be a "wonder worker!"

Personal Notes:

_____

_____

_____

_____

_____

_____

_____

_____

_____

_____

_____

_____

_____

_____

_____

_____

_____

_____

_____

_____

_____

_____

Devotion 22

Three kings were in a world of trouble. At Jehoram's lead, they had taken their armies out into the wilderness, and now everyone was at risk of dying for lack of water. In their hour of desperation, these three kings came looking for help and answers from Elisha the prophet. So, picture the setting. Three "men of the world" coming to a member of the clergy. In that situation, the proper clergical response is always kindness and tenderness, correct?

That would be a "no."

2 Kings 3:13 *And Elisha said unto the king of Israel, What have I to do with thee? get thee to the prophets of thy father, and to the prophets of thy mother. And the king of Israel said unto him, Nay: for the LORD hath called these three kings together, to deliver them into the hand of Moab.* **14** *And Elisha said, As the LORD of hosts liveth, before whom I stand, surely, were it not that I regard the presence of Jehoshaphat the king of Judah, I would not look toward thee, nor see thee.*

Allow me to paraphrase. Jehoram: "We need help!" Elisha: "Go back to your own sorry church and horrible clergy." Jehoram: "But we are going to die if we don't get help!" Elisha: "If you weren't standing beside Jehoshaphat, whom I have a tiny bit of respect for, I wouldn't even look your direction."

Ouch! If Elisha were on Twitter or Facebook, he would get chewed out non-stop for such "un-Christ-likeness." But anyone who did so would be proving that they know little of either Elisha or Christ.

Some preachers today are far too hard. But exponentially more are something much worse—far too soft. No one listening to them ever even realizes their lost or backslidden estate, and their need to repent. They send sinners to hell feeling good about themselves and carnal Christians to the judgment seat of Christ utterly empty-handed, saved so as by fire.

DO be glad for any time a preacher cuts you with the truth! A harsh truth is better than a smooth lie every single time.

Personal Notes:

_____

_____

_____

_____

_____

_____

_____

_____

_____

_____

_____

_____

_____

_____

_____

_____

_____

_____

_____

_____

Devotion 23

Elisha had harshly condemned King Jehoram. But, since King Jehoshaphat was in need as well, he chose to help by seeking a word from God for them. But notice how he did that.

2 Kings 3:15 *But now bring me a minstrel. And it came to pass, when the minstrel played, that the hand of the LORD came upon him.*

A minstrel was a musician, specifically a musician who played stringed instruments. Elisha did not just "spout off his opinion." He sought the hand of the Lord, and he did so by listening to music that would help to make that happen. And notice that there were not even any lyrics involved; it was just music.

For years people have debated the question, "is music amoral?" The answer is no. Music, all by itself, can either carry people toward sinful thoughts and moods or righteous thoughts and moods. Elisha had the hand of the Lord come on him as a result of this music; the multitudes in Babylon were primed to bow to an idol by Nebuchadnezzar's music.

Very few forces on earth are as powerful as music. Sports teams run onto the court to the tune of "eye of the tiger" or something of that nature, not Barney the Dinosaur's "I love you, you love me."

DO, therefore, be very careful of the music you listen to day in and day out. Depression or joy, praise or pouting is likely just a turn of the dial or a click of the app away!

Personal Notes:

_____

_____

_____

_____

_____

_____

_____

_____

_____

_____

_____

_____

_____

_____

_____

_____

_____

_____

_____

_____

_____

_____

_____

_____

_____

_____

_____

Devotion 24

Everyone was in the wilderness about to die of thirst. What solution did God give by the mouth of Elisha? Try "dig a ditch."

2 Kings 3:16 *And he said, Thus saith the LORD, Make this valley full of ditches.*

Ditches. Not wells, ditches. How in the world could that even begin to solve the problem?

2 Kings 3:17 *For thus saith the LORD, Ye shall not see wind, neither shall ye see rain; yet that valley shall be filled with water, that ye may drink, both ye, and your cattle, and your beasts.* **18** *And this is but a light thing in the sight of the LORD: he will deliver the Moabites also into your hand.* **19** *And ye shall smite every fenced city, and every choice city, and shall fell every good tree, and stop all wells of water, and mar every good piece of land with stones.* **20** *And it came to pass in the morning, when the meat offering was offered, that, behold, there came water by the way of Edom, and the country was filled with water.*

This makes no human sense. Without rain, without wind, water came rushing into the valley and filled up all of the ditches everyone had dug. It was a miracle. And it was a miracle that came when people "dug in God's direction." You see, the normal direction to dig for water is down (a well) not sideways (a ditch). But they did not need normal; they needed supernatural. If one needs normal, digging the normal way will work. If one needs supernatural, only digging God's way will work!

DO be willing to "dig" God's way, unless you are content to live a life of "normal!"

Personal Notes:

_____

_____

_____

_____

_____

_____

_____

_____

_____

_____

_____

_____

_____

_____

_____

_____

_____

_____

_____

_____

_____

_____

_____

_____

_____

_____

_____

Devotion 25

The miracle of water gave the three kings the gift of life. But, unbeknownst to them, it would also give them something else—victory.

2 Kings 3:21 *And when all the Moabites heard that the kings were come up to fight against them, they gathered all that were able to put on armour, and upward, and stood in the border. **22** And they rose up early in the morning, and the sun shone upon the water, and the Moabites saw the water on the other side as red as blood: **23** And they said, This is blood: the kings are surely slain, and they have smitten one another: now therefore, Moab, to the spoil. **24** And when they came to the camp of Israel, the Israelites rose up and smote the Moabites, so that they fled before them: but they went forward smiting the Moabites, even in their country.*

Realizing that there were three kings of three different nations banded together to fight them, when the Moabites looked that direction and saw the light bouncing off of the water at just the right angle to make it look blood red, they assumed that their enemies had turned on each other. Because of that, they carelessly rushed in and were beaten soundly by the three kings and their forces.

Had the three kings not gotten into a desperate bind to begin with, they would never have called on God, God would not have sent the miraculous water, and they would have had to fight a normal battle, complete with much loss of life. The problem they found themselves in became the very source of their ultimate victory.

Many times, we find ourselves in desperate situations and wonder why God has let it come to that. But what we often find is that God uses those very situations as the source of our greatest victories.

DO remember to praise Him in the dry, low, times; He never brings us to those times without a very good reason!

Personal Notes:

_____
_____
_____
_____
_____
_____
_____
_____
_____
_____
_____
_____
_____
_____
_____
_____
_____
_____
_____
_____
_____
_____
_____

Devotion 26

Realizing the battle was lost, the king of Moab made one last desperate attempt to escape. It failed. And what followed was barbaric.

2 Kings 3:26 *And when the king of Moab saw that the battle was too sore for him, he took with him seven hundred men that drew swords, to break through even unto the king of Edom: but they could not.* **27** *Then he took his eldest son that should have reigned in his stead, and offered him for a burnt offering upon the wall. And there was great indignation against Israel: and they departed from him, and returned to their own land.*

Behold the basest instincts of pagan mankind. Realizing he was about to die, this king sacrificed his own eldest son to his "gods," and did so up high and out in the open where everyone could see. This turned the view of every surrounding person and nation against Israel, on whom they placed the blame. Realizing that things were about to escalate to epic proportions, Israel left and went home.

A father sacrificed his son to death to appease his so-called gods. Israel took the blame. No mention is made of any "indignation" directed at the man who actually killed his own son.

And isn't that the way mankind usually does it? Do wrong and then pass the buck. Give your own side a pass. Wave pompoms for the jersey of your choice.

What a sorry way to live. DO have enough character to place blame where it belongs, not where it is convenient!

Personal Notes:

_____
_____
_____
_____
_____
_____
_____
_____
_____
_____
_____
_____
_____
_____
_____
_____
_____
_____
_____
_____
_____
_____
_____
_____
_____
_____
_____
_____

Devotion 27

The scene now shifts away from the battlefield and back to Elisha. A "preacher's wife" has become a widow, and her family is now in deep trouble.

2 Kings 4:1 *Now there cried a certain woman of the wives of the sons of the prophets unto Elisha, saying, Thy servant my husband is dead; and thou knowest that thy servant did fear the LORD: and the creditor is come to take unto him my two sons to be bondmen. 2 And Elisha said unto her, What shall I do for thee? tell me, what hast thou in the house? And she said, Thine handmaid hath not any thing in the house, save a pot of oil.*

This woman was able to speak to the character of her dead husband, and it was a good character. Nonetheless, that would not stop the creditors from taking her two sons as bondmen to pay the debt. So, she called out to Elisha for help, and his answer to her was, "What do you have in the house?"

What an interesting question! His solution did not start with "What can I give you," it started with "What do you already have to work with?"

That is actually the proper place to always start looking for a solution. God is very good about providing resources before a disaster. The problem with that is we usually squander rather than save!

DO save, and DO, in any disaster, first ask the question, "What has God already given me to work with?"

Personal Notes:

_____
_____
_____
_____
_____
_____
_____
_____
_____
_____
_____
_____
_____
_____
_____
_____
_____
_____
_____
_____
_____
_____
_____
_____
_____
_____

Devotion 28

After Elisha asked the woman what she had with her in the house, the woman responded that all she had was a pot of oil. No doubt in her mind was the thought, "What good can something so small possibly do?"

But Elisha had just the answer to that unspoken question.

2 Kings 4:3 *Then he said, Go, borrow thee vessels abroad of all thy neighbours, even empty vessels; borrow not a few. 4 And when thou art come in, thou shalt shut the door upon thee and upon thy sons, and shalt pour out into all those vessels, and thou shalt set aside that which is full. 5 So she went from him, and shut the door upon her and upon her sons, who brought the vessels to her; and she poured out. 6 And it came to pass, when the vessels were full, that she said unto her son, Bring me yet a vessel. And he said unto her, There is not a vessel more. And the oil stayed.*

In tomorrow's devotion we will focus on the miracle itself. For today, please just think with me for a second of how odd it must have been for the people of the town to have someone knock on the door and asked to borrow empty containers! People are used to being asked for things, but empty containers are rarely one of those things. Most of the time people want to borrow containers that already have something inside of them: sugar, oil, a casserole, whatever.

Just an empty vessel. That is all anyone was asked to give.

If you ever think an empty vessel is not precious in God's sight, think back on this text. When you find yourself as an empty vessel before the Lord, DO realize that that is exactly what He wants you to give! It is our responsibility to provide the empty vessel, it is God's responsibility to fill it!

Personal Notes:

_____

_____

_____

_____

_____

_____

_____

_____

_____

_____

_____

_____

_____

_____

_____

_____

_____

_____

_____

_____

_____

_____

_____

_____

Devotion 29

The task of borrowing the empty vessels was done. But then came the miracle that would make all of those empty vessels worth so very much.

2 Kings 4:5 *So she went from him, and shut the door upon her and upon her sons, who brought the vessels to her; and she poured out. 6 And it came to pass, when the vessels were full, that she said unto her son, Bring me yet a vessel. And he said unto her, There is not a vessel more. And the oil stayed. 7 Then she came and told the man of God. And he said, Go, sell the oil, and pay thy debt, and live thou and thy children of the rest.*

The debt this family had accumulated was so great that two sons were about to be taken as bondmen to repay it. All the woman had was one pot of oil, nowhere near enough to pay that debt. She took that pot of oil and filled up an empty vessel... then another... then another until there was literally no other vessel left into which to pour it! We could put it this way; her little jug filled up hundreds of gallons of empty vessels! It was enough to pay the entire debt and to support the woman and her children from there on out.

DO remember that we serve a God of miracles, and DO pay attention and be watchful for those special times when He does them!

Personal Notes:

_____
_____
_____
_____
_____
_____
_____
_____
_____
_____
_____
_____
_____
_____
_____
_____
_____
_____
_____
_____
_____
_____
_____
_____
_____
_____

Devotion 30

Sometime after Elisha had helped the widow woman through the miracle of the un-ending supply of oil in the pot, he crossed paths with another woman.

2 Kings 4:8 *And it fell on a day, that Elisha passed to Shunem, where was a great woman; and she constrained him to eat bread. And so it was, that as oft as he passed by, he turned in thither to eat bread.* *9 And she said unto her husband, Behold now, I perceive that this is an holy man of God, which passeth by us continually.* *10 Let us make a little chamber, I pray thee, on the wall; and let us set for him there a bed, and a table, and a stool, and a candlestick: and it shall be, when he cometh to us, that he shall turn in thither.*

You will often hear from God haters and Bible scoffers that, "God and the Bible are misogynistic (hateful toward women) especially in the Old Testament." And yet, time and time again that opinion is proven to be demonstrably false.

The woman in this passage is described as a "great" woman, meaning very important. Her husband is not described that way. It was the woman who orchestrated Elisha's repeated visits to the home, and it was the woman who perceived that Elisha was a holy man of God. It was the woman who suggested making a prophet's chamber for him to stay in whenever he came that way.

If you are looking for a book or religion that is anti-woman, DO look somewhere other than the

Bible or Christianity, because you will not find any of that in God's book or in God's instructions to His people!

Personal Notes:

_____

_____

_____

_____

_____

_____

_____

_____

_____

_____

_____

_____

_____

_____

_____

_____

_____

_____

_____

_____

_____

_____

_____

_____

_____

_____

_____

_____

Devotion 31

The great woman of Shunem had been such a blessing to Elisha and Gehazi. Thinking on that one day, Elisha determined to return the favor.

2 Kings 4:11 *And it fell on a day, that he came thither, and he turned into the chamber, and lay there.* **12** *And he said to Gehazi his servant, Call this Shunammite. And when he had called her, she stood before him.* **13** *And he said unto him, Say now unto her, Behold, thou hast been careful for us with all this care; what is to be done for thee? wouldest thou be spoken for to the king, or to the captain of the host? And she answered, I dwell among mine own people.* **14** *And he said, What then is to be done for her?*

In tomorrow's devotion we will begin to cover Gehazi's answer to Elisha's question. But for now, please meditate for a few moments on the fact that Elisha was determined to be a giver, not just always a receiver.

There are two primary bodies of water inland in the land of Israel. Up north is the sea of Galilee, down south is the Dead Sea, and the Jordan River flows from the former to the latter. The sea of Galilee both receives water and sends water out. The Dead Sea has no major outlet for water. The sea of Galilee is teeming with life; the Dead Sea has no life within it.

DO understand that a life always lived on the receiving end will produce nothing but deadness. Be willing to receive, but be active in giving out as well if you expect to have life instead of mere existence!

Personal Notes:

_____

_____

_____

_____

_____

_____

_____

_____

_____

_____

_____

_____

_____

_____

_____

_____

_____

_____

_____

_____

_____

_____

_____

_____

_____

_____

_____

_____

Devotion 32

When Elisha could not figure out what to do for the great woman of Shunem, his servant, Gehazi, had just the answer: "She has no child, and her husband is old."

Elisha must have smiled at what he was about to tell the woman once he heard that.

2 Kings 4:15 *And he said, Call her. And when he had called her, she stood in the door.* **16** *And he said, About this season, according to the time of life, thou shalt embrace a son. And she said, Nay, my lord, thou man of God, do not lie unto thine handmaid.* **17** *And the woman conceived, and bare a son at that season that Elisha had said unto her, according to the time of life.*

That phrase that is used twice, "according to the time of life," basically means, "the normal term of a pregnancy." In other words, this woman within the next couple of months would get pregnant, and about the same season next year would be holding a child! The woman was shocked at that proclamation, and her words indicate that she was having trouble believing it. And yet, it happened exactly as Elisha had said. God gave her not just the desires of her heart, but the unspoken desires of her heart!

DO take comfort in the fact that God knows what you want even if you have not been brave enough to say it out loud!

Personal Notes:

_____

_____

_____

_____

_____

_____

_____

_____

_____

_____

_____

_____

_____

_____

_____

_____

_____

_____

_____

_____

_____

_____

_____

_____

_____

_____

_____

_____

Devotion 33

The great woman of Shunem had her precious baby boy. But in one verse's time, his childhood is skimmed over and tragedy overtakes him.

2 Kings 4:18 *And when the child was grown, it fell on a day, that he went out to his father to the reapers.* **19** *And he said unto his father, My head, my head. And he said to a lad, Carry him to his mother.* **20** *And when he had taken him, and brought him to his mother, he sat on her knees till noon, and then died.*

My mind is drawn to the father of the child at this point, and not in a good way. I cannot for the life of me gloss over the fact that this boy obviously had something seriously wrong with him, and the father simply had someone else carry the boy to his mother and did not even go with him.

There are some good things we can say about the father. He was obviously a faithful husband, a hard worker, a good provider. And yet he seems to be utterly emotionally distant from the family, especially his own son, even in the greatest hour of need.

Dads, you need to be a faithful husband, a hard worker, and a good provider. But the list should not stop there. DO rise to the final challenge and be actively connected to your family spiritually and emotionally! The bacon is not nearly as important as the man carrying it home!

Personal Notes:

_____
_____
_____
_____
_____
_____
_____
_____
_____
_____
_____
_____
_____
_____
_____
_____
_____
_____
_____
_____
_____
_____
_____
_____
_____
_____
_____
_____
_____

Devotion 34

The child was dead, the father was either disinterested or oblivious, and all seemed lost. But, remember, in the words of Scripture we are dealing with a "great woman," not a run-of-the-mill person. And she was about to show another facet of her greatness.

2 Kings 4:22-23 *And she called unto her husband, and said, Send me, I pray thee, one of the young men, and one of the asses, that I may run to the man of God, and come again. And he said, Wherefore wilt thou go to him to day? it is neither new moon, nor sabbath. And she said, It shall be well.*

Pay attention to those words, "It shall be well," and remember that her son was still very much dead as she said them.

As she traveled toward Elisha and got near to Mt. Carmel, Elisha saw her coming and sent his servant out to meet her with some questions. Notice how that exchange went:

2 Kings 4:26 *Run now, I pray thee, to meet her, and say unto her, Is it well with thee? is it well with thy husband? is it well with the child? And she answered, It is well.*

Do you see the change? "It shall be well" has now become "It is well!" Her circumstances had not changed, but her faith had grown stronger in spite of that. And since the present and the future could not be the source of that growing faith, it could only be the past out of which it grew. This woman had no assurances of what, if anything, God would do in this

72

particular circumstance, but she did remember and lay hold on all that He had already done in other circumstances, and as such, she could confidently say, "It is well."

DO be in the habit of remembering all that God has already done for you in the past. That is the fertile soil out of which "It is well" grows in the present!

Personal Notes:

_____

_____

_____

_____

_____

_____

_____

_____

_____

_____

_____

_____

_____

_____

_____

_____

_____

_____

_____

_____

_____

_____

Devotion 35

The great woman of Shunem had finally gotten to Elisha and was about to pour her broken heart out to him. When she did, something very interesting came to light, something that gives us a bit of insight into the workings of God.

2 Kings 4:27 *And when she came to the man of God to the hill, she caught him by the feet: but Gehazi came near to thrust her away. And the man of God said, Let her alone; for her soul is vexed within her: and the LORD hath hid it from me, and hath not told me.*

Gehazi had no clue what was going on; he just knew that this woman was grabbing at the feet of his master, and he wanted to get her off of him. But Elisha instantly knew that something was very wrong and stopped him. It is then that Elisha said, "*Let her alone; for her soul is vexed within her: and the LORD hath hid it from me, and hath not told me.*"

Question: did God know? Yes, of course He knew. Question number two: could God have told Elisha? Yes, He could have told him every single detail before the woman ever arrived. In fact, He did that very thing in 1 Kings 14 with the wife of Jeroboam when her son Abijah got sick!

So why did God not tell Elisha? The simple answer is because He didn't have to and didn't want to. The fact that God CAN do everything does not mean that he HAS TO do anything! In this particular case, God hiding this from Elisha ended up setting the stage for one of the greatest miracles of the Old Testament.

DO trust that God can do everything, but DO also trust Him even if He does not seem to do anything!

Personal Notes:

_____

_____

_____

_____

_____

_____

_____

_____

_____

_____

_____

_____

_____

_____

_____

_____

_____

_____

_____

_____

_____

_____

_____

_____

_____

_____

Devotion 36

Fixed at the feet of Elisha, the great woman of Shunem poured out her heart. She hearkened back in time to the words she spoke to Elisha many years earlier when he told her she would have a child:

2 Kings 4:28 *Then she said, Did I desire a son of my lord? did I not say, Do not deceive me?*

Those were all the words that Elisha needed to hear to know that the child had died. So he determined to do something about it.

2 Kings 4:29 *Then he said to Gehazi, Gird up thy loins, and take my staff in thine hand, and go thy way: if thou meet any man, salute him not; and if any salute thee, answer him not again: and lay my staff upon the face of the child.*

Elisha was sending Gehazi to try and raise the boy back to life. And we will get to that tomorrow. But for now, it is the instructions that he gave him from point A to point B in which we find a valuable lesson for life. Elisha told Gehazi not to even stop and speak to anyone along the way, even if they spoke to him first. Now, how do you think others must have reacted to that? How must Isaac, the camel merchant, have felt when he spoke to Gehazi, and Gehazi simply ignored him and kept right on moving? How must Abigail, the cloth weaver, have reacted when she called out to him by name and he did not even turn his head that direction?

There were doubtless many that thought him rude and perhaps even some that talked about him in the worst way for years afterward. But Gehazi had a very good reason to do what he was doing; every second was critical, and he could not take any time to explain that.

DO give good people something very precious—the benefit of the doubt! When all the facts of any situation are finally known, you may well be glad that you did!

Personal Notes:

_____

_____

_____

_____

_____

_____

_____

_____

_____

_____

_____

_____

_____

_____

_____

_____

_____

_____

_____

_____

_____

_____

_____

_____

Devotion 37

Elisha had sent Gehazi on ahead to try and raise her son. But for the great woman of Shunem, that was not enough, not at all.

2 Kings 4:30 *And the mother of the child said, As the LORD liveth, and as thy soul liveth, I will not leave thee. And he arose, and followed her.*

This woman was a remarkable mother. She was utterly relentless when it came to the welfare of her child. And, as it turns out, she was correct, and the true hero of the story.

2 Kings 4:31 *And Gehazi passed on before them, and laid the staff upon the face of the child; but there was neither voice, nor hearing. Wherefore he went again to meet him, and told him, saying, The child is not awaked.*

Gehazi was not able to raise the child. Gehazi was not the prophet of God. Had the mother not insisted that Elisha himself come, all would have been lost. But at her insistence he did come, and here is the end of the story:

2 Kings 4:36 *And he called Gehazi, and said, Call this Shunammite. So he called her. And when she was come in unto him, he said, Take up thy son.* **37** *Then she went in, and fell at his feet, and bowed herself to the ground, and took up her son, and went out.*

This mother was not the one who raised her son, but she is the one who caused him to be raised by her relentless persistence. Parents, DO be relentless in everything that matters concerning your children;

there are substitutes for many things in life, but there is no substitute for persistence!

Personal Notes:

_____

_____

_____

_____

_____

_____

_____

_____

_____

_____

_____

_____

_____

_____

_____

_____

_____

_____

_____

_____

_____

_____

_____

_____

_____

_____

_____

Devotion 38

Sometime after raising the son of the great woman of Shunem from the dead, Elisha made his way over to Gilgal. This is where the "prophets in training" were gathered. And, like most "preacher boys," they were hungry and anxious for a meal.

2 Kings 4:38 *And Elisha came again to Gilgal: and there was a dearth in the land; and the sons of the prophets were sitting before him: and he said unto his servant, Set on the great pot, and seethe pottage for the sons of the prophets.* **39** *And one went out into the field to gather herbs, and found a wild vine, and gathered thereof wild gourds his lap full, and came and shred them into the pot of pottage: for they knew them not.* **40** *So they poured out for the men to eat. And it came to pass, as they were eating of the pottage, that they cried out, and said, O thou man of God, there is death in the pot. And they could not eat thereof.*

Does anyone out there want a quick cooking lesson? Here you go. Cooking 101: don't throw random, unknown ingredients into the pot, especially things that you found growing in the field and have no idea what they are. One of these guys did just that, and as they were putting the pottage into their mouths, someone realized that whatever had been put in was poison!

It was just one ingredient, but that one ingredient was going to kill everyone.

DO be careful of every ingredient in "the casserole that is your life." One poison attitude, one poison secret sin, one poison friendship, one poison choice, one poison anything can destroy you, no matter how good and wholesome the rest of the ingredients are!

Personal Notes:

_____

_____

_____

_____

_____

_____

_____

_____

_____

_____

_____

_____

_____

_____

_____

_____

_____

_____

_____

_____

_____

_____

_____

_____

_____

_____

_____

Devotion 39

Elisha dealt with the poison pottage in our last devotion, healing it, as it were, and making it fit for everyone to eat. But the very next thing we read of was another food problem.

2 Kings 4:42 *And there came a man from Baalshalisha, and brought the man of God bread of the firstfruits, twenty loaves of barley, and full ears of corn in the husk thereof. And he said, Give unto the people, that they may eat.* **43** *And his servitor said, What, should I set this before an hundred men?*

A man came to Elisha with food. Specifically, he came with twenty barley loaves and some corn. If that sounds like a lot, trust me, it wasn't. Do you remember how many of these loaves a simple boy later packed for his lunch?

John 6:9 *There is a lad here, which hath five barley loaves, and two small fishes: but what are they among so many?*

So, if five barley loaves were a meal for one, twenty barley loaves were roughly a meal for four. And yet Elisha told the man to go ahead and set that out for everyone. Not surprisingly, as we have seen, he was incredulous. Yet here is what Elisha told him.

2 Kings 4:43... *Give the people, that they may eat: for thus saith the LORD, They shall eat, and shall leave thereof.*

And they did.

2 Kings 4:44 *So he set it before them, and they did eat, and left thereof, according to the word of the LORD.*

This was a miniature feeding of the 5,000 hundreds of years before the time of Christ. What God did in small measure through Elisha, He did in full measure through Christ.

DO realize that, when it comes to Christ, it will always be a matter of "You think that's great? You ain't seen nothing yet!"

Personal Notes:

_____
_____
_____
_____
_____
_____
_____
_____
_____
_____
_____
_____
_____
_____
_____
_____
_____
_____
_____
_____
_____
_____
_____
_____
_____

Devotion 40

As we enter into 2 Kings 5, a new character bursts onto the scene, one of the most colorful characters of the Old Testament.

2 Kings 5:1 *Now Naaman, captain of the host of the king of Syria, was a great man with his master, and honourable, because by him the LORD had given deliverance unto Syria: he was also a mighty man in valour...*

The Syrians were the enemies of Israel. They had recently killed Ahab, king of Israel, and it had apparently been Naaman that led that charge. He was the hero of his country, adored by his king, and the words "a mighty man of valor" indicate that he was a huge, strong, fearsome human being. In short, Naaman had life by the tail.

But the verse has one more phrase in it, "*But he was a leper.*"

Naaman had it all, and yet had nothing. He was living large, and yet dying horribly. He was adored, and yet no one really wanted to be near him.

It is things like that that ought to make us evaluate our priorities.

DO take stock of your life. If you are saved, healthy, and still have family, you are richer than most people living miserably in their mansions, on their way to hell, hooked on drugs, and with nothing but the shallowest of relationships!

Personal Notes:

Devotion 41

In verse one we were introduced to mighty Naaman. But in verse two we will be introduced to someone far superior to him in every way that could possibly matter.

2 Kings 5:2 *And the Syrians had gone out by companies, and had brought away captive out of the land of Israel a little maid; and she waited on Naaman's wife.*

Nowhere in Scripture are we given this precious girl's name. But we are told that she was taken captive from the land of Israel. She was even then a bondslave in the house of Naaman, whose people had ravaged her land and likely killed everyone she loved in the process.

Put yourself in her place. How would you feel if you learned that your captor, Naaman, had leprosy and was dying? Don't be pious; you and I both know that you would likely be celebrating, and probably using the word "karma" a lot...

But not this girl. She genuinely cared for Naaman and did not want to see him die such a horrible death. Not to get too far ahead of ourselves, but her concern did not just save Naaman's life, but his soul as well! Naaman is in heaven today all because of a young girl who showed love when no one would have faulted her for hating him.

DO remember that every person you meet is a precious soul that will spend eternity either in heaven or in hell, and you may be the very one God has chosen to love them toward salvation!

Personal Notes:

_____
_____
_____
_____
_____
_____
_____
_____
_____
_____
_____
_____
_____
_____
_____
_____
_____
_____
_____
_____
_____
_____
_____
_____
_____
_____
_____

Devotion 42

In our last devotion we were introduced to a precious young lady whom I told you had a genuine concern for Naaman. Now we will begin to see not just her concern, but also something equally if not even more remarkable.

2 Kings 5:3 *And she said unto her mistress, Would God my lord were with the prophet that is in Samaria! for he would recover him of his leprosy.*

Reading at a normal pace, if you started at Genesis 1:1 and read straight through to 2 Kings 5:3, it would take the average reader right around 24 hours to do so. And if you did, let me tell you what you would not find a single instance of in all of that 24 hours, not in one single verse—any human being healing someone of leprosy.

It simply had never been done! And yet this little girl had such confidence in Elisha, the man of God, that she told her mistress that if Naaman would go see Elisha, Elisha would recover him of his leprosy!

This little girl understood, as did any spiritual person, that Elisha's power did not come from himself, but from God. So, though her confidence was in Elisha, her faith was in God. She was willing to believe God for things that no one in humanity's history had ever yet seen.

What an example! Anyone can believe something they have become accustomed to, but faith in God is able to believe even the things that have not yet even been seen.

DO have a faith that goes beyond things you have come to expect; the God we are trusting is infinite, not finite!

Personal Notes:

_____

_____

_____

_____

_____

_____

_____

_____

_____

_____

_____

_____

_____

_____

_____

_____

_____

_____

_____

_____

_____

_____

_____

_____

_____

_____

_____

Devotion 43

The little maid had been very, very specific about who could heal Naaman and what office he held: Elisha, prophet. Well, someone overheard those words and relayed them to the king of Syria. And that began one of the most hilarious, "politicians can mess up anything" situations in human history.

2 Kings 5:5 *And the king of Syria said, Go to, go, and I will send a letter unto the king of Israel. And he departed, and took with him ten talents of silver, and six thousand pieces of gold, and ten changes of raiment.* **6** *And he brought the letter to the king of Israel, saying, Now when this letter is come unto thee, behold, I have therewith sent Naaman my servant to thee, that thou mayest recover him of his leprosy.* **7** *And it came to pass, when the king of Israel had read the letter, that he rent his clothes, and said, Am I God, to kill and to make alive, that this man doth send unto me to recover a man of his leprosy? wherefore consider, I pray you, and see how he seeketh a quarrel against me.*

Long story short, two nations almost duked it out over a misplaced communique! No kings should have even been involved in this. The only person who was needed was the preacher, Elisha.

But isn't that the way political types and their ardent followers, tend to think? All problems can be solved by another vote, a treaty, a backroom deal?

DO remember a few things. One, some problems can only be solved by God. Two, politicians, *ahem*, cannot always be trusted to get things right. And three, always send your notes to the right people!

Personal Notes:

_____

_____

_____

_____

_____

_____

_____

_____

_____

_____

_____

_____

_____

_____

_____

_____

_____

_____

_____

_____

_____

_____

_____

_____

_____

Devotion 44

When the king of Israel got the unexpected and seemingly provocative letter from the king of Syria, he went ballistic. He was scared to death and whining like a petulant child. He even went so far as to tear his clothes! Well, with the king making that kind of a scene, it was not long till Elisha himself heard of it.

2 Kings 5:8 *And it was so, when Elisha the man of God had heard that the king of Israel had rent his clothes, that he sent to the king, saying, Wherefore hast thou rent thy clothes? let him come now to me, and he shall know that there is a prophet in Israel.*

One of the popular things in our day is "proud humility." By that I mean that people often wear their "humility" as a badge of pride! I have seen them go so far as to say that preachers should never use terms like "man of God," because how dare we be so proud to say such a thing! This, mind you, despite the fact that that phrase is found seventy-eight times in Scripture!

For Elisha, the title was "prophet." It was his God-given office, and he did not shy away from the title or from the authority that came with it. And that is good, because Naaman did not need an annoying "humility celebrity;" he needed someone who knew what God had made him to be and was willing to be just that.

Whether pastor, parent, officer, business owner, whatever God has made you to be, it is not pride to say so and act it; it is a notice to the needy that they can come to you with confidence. So DO unashamedly and openly be what God has made you to be!

Personal Notes:

_____
_____
_____
_____
_____
_____
_____
_____
_____
_____
_____
_____
_____
_____
_____
_____
_____
_____
_____
_____
_____
_____
_____
_____
_____
_____
_____

Devotion 45

Naaman finally got the word that, though the king of Israel could not help him, the prophet of Israel could. So off he went to Elisha's house. And when he got there, it only took a few seconds for there to be a very predictable standoff.

2 Kings 5:9 *So Naaman came with his horses and with his chariot, and stood at the door of the house of Elisha. 10 And Elisha sent a messenger unto him, saying, Go and wash in Jordan seven times, and thy flesh shall come again to thee, and thou shalt be clean. 11 But Naaman was wroth, and went away, and said, Behold, I thought, He will surely come out to me, and stand, and call on the name of the LORD his God, and strike his hand over the place, and recover the leper.*

Clearly, Naaman and Elisha were butting heads right off the bat. Naaman sat proud in his chariot outside the door and waited for the "lowly man of God" to come out and, in awe of great Naaman, perform a miracle and heal him. Elisha, though, sat right where he was in his house. He did not even bother to show Naaman his face, he just sent a messenger out with the instructions, "Go take seven baths in the river and you will be fine."

Naaman was livid: "How DARE he!"

Fill in the blank for me in your mind. This was a standoff between Naaman the _____ and Elisha the _____. In Naaman's mind, he would have filled in the blanks with something like "general" and "prophet." But I hope you didn't, because the accurate terms would be "LEPER" and "prophet!" Naaman was dying as a leper, while strutting as a general! And that pride was literally going to kill him if he did not let it go.

DO remember that we all stand before God as needy sinners and then as needy saints!

Personal Notes:

_____

_____

_____

_____

_____

_____

_____

_____

_____

_____

_____

_____

_____

_____

_____

_____

_____

_____

_____

_____

_____

_____

_____

Devotion 46

Naaman's lethal pride came from many things. But one unusual source of it at this point was a couple of rivers. Naaman had been instructed by Elisha to go wash seven times in the Jordan river. And while baptistery paintings of "the Jordan" through the years have always showed a lovely blue river meandering peacefully past the swaying palm trees, that picture is simply not reality—the Jordan is a muddy river!

But back home, there was something "better" in Naaman's estimation:

2 Kings 5:12 *Are not Abana and Pharpar, rivers of Damascus, better than all the waters of Israel? may I not wash in them, and be clean? So he turned and went away in a rage.*

The Abana and Pharpar Rivers were legendary for their beauty and healthiness. Those rivers would be far more suitable for a great man like Naaman to wash in, according to Naaman the dying leper!

What a picture this is of salvation! God has made a way through His Son suffering and dying on a rugged cross and our bowing before Him in humility and repentance to receive Him as Lord and Savior. But the world looks at that and says, "Behold, here are the sacraments, or baptismal regeneration, or confirmation, or being good; may I not do these and be saved?"

And the answer is no. There was only one river Naaman could wash in and be clean, and there is only one way of salvation. Elisha would not direct this dying man to something he was "comfortable with" when he knew good and well it would never work!

DO become familiar with the number "one," because that is exactly how many ways there are to be saved!

Personal Notes:

_____

_____

_____

_____

_____

_____

_____

_____

_____

_____

_____

_____

_____

_____

_____

_____

_____

_____

_____

_____

_____

_____

_____

_____

Devotion 47

Naaman heard what Elisha said, and his response was to leave in a rage. Now, in the mercy of God, it had been an unnamed, captive little maid who had directed Naaman to Elisha to begin with. And that same God had, once again in mercy, provided for some other unnamed heroes to pick up the baton at this point.

2 Kings 5:13 *And his servants came near, and spake unto him, and said, My father, if the prophet had bid thee do some great thing, wouldest thou not have done it? how much rather then, when he saith to thee, Wash, and be clean?*

We do not know the name of a single one of these servants. But whoever they were they went to him in his rage, spoke kindly and respectfully to him, and in unassailable logic said words that he could not deny. If Elisha had asked him to crawl across broken glass or scale the highest mountain to be healed, he would have done it. So why would he refuse to do something as simple as "wash and be clean?"

Not to get too far ahead of things, Naaman did just that and more. He did not just get cleansed, he also got saved!

Naaman was richly rewarded for his accomplishments on earth. But when reward day comes in heaven, there will be a simple servant girl and some humble servant guys whom Naaman bows before and says, "Thank you for what you did!"

DO refuse to fret if you are not famous here on earth. In heaven, every simple soul-winner will be an eternal hero!

Personal Notes:

_____

_____

_____

_____

_____

_____

_____

_____

_____

_____

_____

_____

_____

_____

_____

_____

_____

_____

_____

_____

_____

_____

_____

_____

_____

_____

_____

Devotion 48

Naaman's pride finally broke, and he determined to do as he had been told. Elisha had instructed him to dip seven times in the Jordan River, so to the Jordan River he went.

2 Kings 5:14 *Then went he down, and dipped himself seven times in Jordan, according to the saying of the man of God: and his flesh came again like unto the flesh of a little child, and he was clean.*

There is nothing, positively nothing about river water of any kind, anywhere, that can turn the flesh of a leper into the healthy flesh of a little child. The miracle was not in the water; the miracle was in the God who made the water. The vehicle through which God sent that miracle was the faith that Naaman finally exercised in what he had been told.

You see, faith is not a matter of "feeling like you believe." Faith is a matter of belief that leads to action regardless of how you feel. Naaman probably did not "feel" like this was going to work, but he put one foot in front of the other and walked out into the water and dipped seven times and was cleansed of his leprosy.

Many times, Christians doubt their salvation. And when they do, it is most always caused by them trying to remember "how they felt" about the prayer they were praying. Did they mean it enough? Were they sorry enough for their sins? But you see, Elisha did not tell Naaman to wash in the Jordan and feel good about it as he did; he just told him to wash in the Jordan!

DO understand that your feelings have nothing to do with salvation. Until the moment you get saved, your feelings are the feelings of a sinner anyway! Your salvation was paid for in full by Christ on Calvary, and just as the flowing waters of the Jordan carried away the leprosy of Naaman, the blood that flowed down the old, rugged cross carried away your sins the moment you came to Christ for salvation!

Personal Notes:

_____

_____

_____

_____

_____

_____

_____

_____

_____

_____

_____

_____

_____

_____

_____

_____

_____

_____

_____

_____

Devotion 49

When Naaman had arrived at Elisha's house, to say that he was proud, haughty, and arrogant would be an epic understatement. But after he came up out of the Jordan, it wasn't just his body that was changed, but also his heart.

2 Kings 5:15 *And he returned to the man of God, he and all his company, and came, and stood before him: and he said, Behold, now I know that there is no God in all the earth, but in Israel: now therefore, I pray thee, take a blessing of thy servant.*

See how humble Naaman has now become! He is renouncing the gods of Syria, acknowledging the God of Israel, asking to please be allowed to give Elisha financial compensation for what he has done, and calling himself the servant of Elisha.

Nothing changes a person's attitude as thoroughly as coming to know the one true God.

Our society is much like leprous Naaman right now—dying in sin and yet as proud as a peacock. And if we ever expect to change their attitudes, we must understand that neither argument nor reasoning will ever thoroughly do the job. It is only when we introduce people to the God who made them that they are changed from the inside out, so DO tell the world about Him!

Personal Notes:

_____
_____
_____
_____
_____
_____
_____
_____
_____
_____
_____
_____
_____
_____
_____
_____
_____
_____
_____
_____
_____
_____
_____
_____
_____
_____
_____

Devotion 50

Naaman had made what seems to be a very reasonable suggestion. He wanted to give the man of God financial compensation for what he had done. And, since Elisha had literally saved his life and led him to the saving of his soul, it certainly would be worth everything that Naaman could do and infinitely more! And yet, look at the firm answer of Elisha to that question:

2 Kings 5:15 *And he returned to the man of God, he and all his company, and came, and stood before him: and he said, Behold, now I know that there is no God in all the earth, but in Israel: now therefore, I pray thee, take a blessing of thy servant.* **16** *But he said, As the LORD liveth, before whom I stand, I will receive none. And he urged him to take it; but he refused.*

In many other places in Scripture, we find God's men willingly receiving compensation for the things they did. So why, in this particular case, did Elisha refuse?

The heathen priests of the Gentiles eagerly and greedily received money for their services, even though what they did was of no worth whatsoever. Had Elisha received the money from Naaman, he would have appeared to be on the same level as them. But even worse than that, His God would have appeared to be on the same level as their false gods! So, for the sake of the lost who were watching, at this time he refused.

That is called discernment and discretion.

DO pay careful attention to every situation, because what may be acceptable for you to do in one situation may actually be completely unacceptable in a different situation!

Personal Notes:

_____

_____

_____

_____

_____

_____

_____

_____

_____

_____

_____

_____

_____

_____

_____

_____

_____

_____

_____

_____

_____

_____

_____

_____

_____

_____

Devotion 51

After Elisha refused the financial gift of Naaman, we come to what seems to be one of the oddest exchanges in the Bible.

2 Kings 5:17 *And Naaman said, Shall there not then, I pray thee, be given to thy servant two mules' burden of earth? for thy servant will henceforth offer neither burnt offering nor sacrifice unto other gods, but unto the LORD.*

In case you wonder whether or not you are reading that right, let me assure you, you are. Naaman literally asked for dirt from Israel to take home with him! Spoiler alert: they had plenty of dirt in Syria! So why in the world was he asking to take dirt home with him? He actually answered that question at the end of the verse when he spoke of offering burnt offering and sacrifice unto the LORD. The heathen nations built elaborate, ornate altars. At God's command, the Israelites built simple altars made of dirt and/or stone. So Naaman wanted Jewish dirt on which to worship the one true God. It was an acknowledgment that everything was better in "God's land," even the dirt!

We often complain about how hard our lot is as Christians. But may I give you a helpful reminder? DO remember that the hardest of the hard days as a Christian is still better than anything that the devil has to offer!

Personal Notes:

_____

_____

_____

_____

_____

_____

_____

_____

_____

_____

_____

_____

_____

_____

_____

_____

_____

_____

_____

_____

_____

_____

_____

_____

_____

_____

_____

Devotion 52

Naaman was done with his request, asking for Jewish dirt to take back home with him. But he was not yet done speaking. And it is in the next thing that he says and the response that Elisha gave that we find an incredibly helpful bit of guidance for today.

2 Kings 5:18 *In this thing the LORD pardon thy servant, that when my master goeth into the house of Rimmon to worship there, and he leaneth on my hand, and I bow myself in the house of Rimmon: when I bow down myself in the house of Rimmon, the LORD pardon thy servant in this thing.* **19** *And he said unto him, Go in peace. So he departed from him a little way.*

Naaman had proclaimed his faith in Jehovah God. But the next thing he said was that he wanted the LORD to "pardon him" in a small matter. When his king, the king of Syria, went to worship in the house of Rimmon, the Syrian god of wind and rain and storms, he required Naaman to be there with him. Apparently, he was frail, for he leaned on Naaman for physical support.

Elisha's answer to that was, "go in peace."

Think about that. Naaman was, in our vernacular, a "brand-new believer." And he was signaling his intention to do something that, quite honestly, he should not have been doing. He was not going to be worshiping Rimmon himself; if he had said that he was going to do that, Elisha definitely would have corrected him. But even going into the house of Rimmon was not something for a believer to do. And yet Elisha did something that many people today forget to do; he gave that new believer space and time to grow.

DO bear in mind, you that have been saved for a while, that brand-new Christians do not know everything yet, nor will they get everything right immediately. So DO lovingly correct anything urgent that needs to be corrected, but DO also give them time and space to grow, time and space for the Lord to work on their heart on things that you perhaps already know!

Personal Notes:

_____

_____

_____

_____

_____

_____

_____

_____

_____

_____

_____

_____

_____

_____

_____

_____

_____

_____

_____

Devotion 53

The little maid of 2 Kings 5 did right. Naaman eventually humbled himself and did right. Elisha did right. But, alas, the account does not end there. After Elisha refused to take any monetary compensation from Naaman, Naaman headed home. But pretty quickly thereafter, someone came chasing after him.

2 Kings 5:20 *But Gehazi, the servant of Elisha the man of God, said, Behold, my master hath spared Naaman this Syrian, in not receiving at his hands that which he brought: but, as the LORD liveth, I will run after him, and take somewhat of him.* **21** *So Gehazi followed after Naaman. And when Naaman saw him running after him, he lighted down from the chariot to meet him, and said, Is all well?* **22** *And he said, All is well. My master hath sent me, saying, Behold, even now there be come to me from mount Ephraim two young men of the sons of the prophets: give them, I pray thee, a talent of silver, and two changes of garments.* **23** *And Naaman said, Be content, take two talents. And he urged him, and bound two talents of silver in two bags, with two changes of garments, and laid them upon two of his servants; and they bare them before him.* **24** *And when he came to the tower, he took them from their hand, and bestowed them in the house: and he let the men go, and they departed.*

Bluntly, Gehazi lied, disobeyed, and stole. And in so doing, he undermined the essential message that Elisha was driving home to Naaman by refusing the money to begin with. Naaman should have been able to go home and tell everyone in Syria about how a real man of God healed him and introduced him to the real God and did not take a penny for his services. But instead, he went back home to Syria with a very different story.

DO remember that there is something much more important than money, namely our testimony and the name of God. Guard both of those things carefully!

Personal Notes:

_____

_____

_____

_____

_____

_____

_____

_____

_____

_____

_____

_____

_____

_____

_____

_____

_____

_____

_____

_____

_____

_____

Devotion 54

Gehazi had hidden his ill-gotten gains, and, satisfied in the belief that no one would ever know, went to stand before Elisha. Alas, he was in for quite a rude awakening.

2 Kings 5:25 *But he went in, and stood before his master. And Elisha said unto him, Whence comest thou, Gehazi? And he said, Thy servant went no whither.* **26** *And he said unto him, Went not mine heart with thee, when the man turned again from his chariot to meet thee? Is it a time to receive money, and to receive garments, and oliveyards, and vineyards, and sheep, and oxen, and menservants, and maidservants?* **27** *The leprosy therefore of Naaman shall cleave unto thee, and unto thy seed for ever. And he went out from his presence a leper as white as snow.*

May I paraphrase? "Gehazi, do you jealously want what Naaman has? Then you shall have it; you shall have all of it. You have taken his silver and clothing, you intended therewith to buy lands and livestock and the ability to gain even more wealth. But if you are going to lie and cheat and steal and take from Naaman what I told him we would not take, and if you are going to go so far as to make it sound like it was my idea, the prophet of God to whom he came for help, then you are also going to have Naaman's leprosy. You will have it, your family will have it, as long as you have descendants, they will have the awful disease from which Naaman has been delivered."

And instantly, Gehazi was a leper, as white as snow. In an instant of time, he gained what his lust desired, and in a second instant of time, he gained what he would wish upon no one.

DO remember that bad gains usually come with bad consequences built in! Be honest, have integrity, and spare yourself and your family the fallout of jealousy and greed!

Personal Notes:

_____

_____

_____

_____

_____

_____

_____

_____

_____

_____

_____

_____

_____

_____

_____

_____

_____

_____

_____

_____

_____

_____

_____

Devotion 55

As we enter into 2 Kings 6, we are for the tenth time in the books of 1 and 2 Kings introduced to a group of people called "the sons of the prophets." They were basically preachers in training. And despite the fact that wicked Jehoram was king and his even more wicked mother Jezebel was still alive and apparently had lost none of her authority, this group of up-and-coming ministers was flourishing. So much so that they had a pleasant problem to deal with:

2 Kings 6:1 *And the sons of the prophets said unto Elisha, Behold now, the place where we dwell with thee is too strait for us. **2** Let us go, we pray thee, unto Jordan, and take thence every man a beam, and let us make us a place there, where we may dwell. And he answered, Go ye. **3** And one said, Be content, I pray thee, and go with thy servants. And he answered, I will go.*

These young men were asking Elisha for permission to move to another location and build a bigger dormitory for them to stay in, as the place where they were then staying was not big enough for all of them. Elisha answered with "go ye."

That is not what they wanted to hear. Yes, they wanted to move and build, but not without Elisha! So, they got a bit more specific and asked him to come with them, a request that he agreed to.

I think some times we "move and grow" without realizing the important things and people we carelessly leave behind. DO take stock of the important people in your life, and as you move and grow, do your best to bring them along with you!

Personal Notes:

_____

_____

_____

_____

_____

_____

_____

_____

_____

_____

_____

_____

_____

_____

_____

_____

_____

_____

_____

_____

_____

_____

_____

_____

_____

_____

Devotion 56

As the prophets in training arrived at Jordan to begin the building process, we come to one of the most unique miracles in all the Bible.

2 Kings 6:4 *So he went with them. And when they came to Jordan, they cut down wood. **5** But as one was felling a beam, the axe head fell into the water: and he cried, and said, Alas, master! for it was borrowed. **6** And the man of God said, Where fell it? And he shewed him the place. And he cut down a stick, and cast it in thither; and the iron did swim. **7** Therefore said he, Take it up to thee. And he put out his hand, and took it.*

I cannot help but to hear a sports announcer's voice here, "And here comes Michael Phelps in lane three, looking like a shoo-in for another gold medal in the 400-meter breaststroke. But wait, gaining on him in lane five is...is.. an axe head! Yes! The axe head has passed Phelps, this is unbelievable, it's the ax head for the gold!"

In all seriousness, the ax head really did swim. And that is a phenomenal miracle. But it is what preceded that miracle that is of particular instance to me. No, not the fact that "a preacher boy lost his power," though I have heard roughly ten thousand (mostly good) messages on that. To me the most interesting thing is that it was not his power to begin with; it was a borrowed ax!

DO understand that if you are living day by day on borrowed spiritual power, whether from a pastor or parent or anyone, that power is likely to fail you at the worst possible time, and you will have no control of it, since it is not your power to begin with. So, DO develop your own power with God!

Personal Notes:

_____

_____

_____

_____

_____

_____

_____

_____

_____

_____

_____

_____

_____

_____

_____

_____

_____

_____

_____

_____

_____

_____

_____

_____

_____

_____

Devotion 57

Things in Old Testament days, especially the way kings and nations behaved, were often really odd. For instance, the king of Syria had sent his chief general, Naaman, to Israel to be healed, and he had come back healed. And yet we will now see the king of Syria coming against Israel to war! Some gratitude, huh? But when he began to lay his plans, a snag developed for him.

2 Kings 6:8 *Then the king of Syria warred against Israel, and took counsel with his servants, saying, In such and such a place shall be my camp.* **9** *And the man of God sent unto the king of Israel, saying, Beware that thou pass not such a place; for thither the Syrians are come down.* **10** *And the king of Israel sent to the place which the man of God told him and warned him of, and saved himself there, not once nor twice.* **11** *Therefore the heart of the king of Syria was sore troubled for this thing; and he called his servants, and said unto them, Will ye not shew me which of us is for the king of Israel?*

In modern terms, the king of Syria realized that he had "a leak." He had only discussed his plans in private with a handful of trusted people, and yet the information was clearly getting out to the king of Israel! This was like an early version of some spy movie.

But there was someone there who knew what was really happening. When the king asked who the leaker was, here was the answer he was given.

2 Kings 6:12 *And one of his servants said, None, my lord, O king: but Elisha, the prophet that is in Israel, telleth the king of Israel the words that thou speakest in thy bedchamber.*

Let's do some investigative work, shall we? Since no one in Syria was in Israel to see or hear or have any idea what Elisha knew or to whom he was telling it, then clearly someone there had had some dealings with Elisha and simply knew what he was capable of!

This seems very much to have been either Naaman or one of the servants that had been with him when Elisha healed him. Someone knew that Elisha had a God that had no trouble seeing everything, hearing everything, and knowing everything.

DO take confidence today knowing that we serve a very big God with limitless ability!

Personal Notes:

_____

_____

_____

_____

_____

_____

_____

_____

_____

_____

_____

_____

_____

Devotion 58

When the king of Syria heard that it was Elisha the prophet that was continually and miraculously telling the king of Israel all of his battle plans, he immediately came up with a "brilliant" solution.

2 Kings 6:13 *And he said, Go and spy where he is, that I may send and fetch him. And it was told him, saying, Behold, he is in Dothan.* **14** *Therefore sent he thither horses, and chariots, and a great host: and they came by night, and compassed the city about.*

The king's solution? "Let's send a gang and kidnap Elisha!"

There is an actor named Liam Neeson. He starred in the "Taken" movies in which members of his family were kidnapped, and he ripped everybody apart going to get them back. He has, in his career, played the role of a Jedi knight, Hannibal Smith of the A-Team, been one of Batman's worst enemies, and even voiced Aslan the Lion in the Chronicles of Narnia movies. Someone recently put together a cute meme that said, "He trained Obi-Wan Kenobi, led the A-Team, nearly killed Batman, and is literally Aslan the Lion. So, what part of kidnaping his family seemed like a good idea?"

The Bible gives us a better one than that, though. It goes something like, "He was trained by Elijah, parted the waters of the Jordan river, raised a dead boy to life, gave a guy and all of his family leprosy, and made an ax head do the back stroke. So, what part of kidnaping him seemed like a good idea?"

As we will see in the next devotion, it wasn't. At all.

DO make wise choices. The only other option, as one modern wag put it is, "Play stupid games, win stupid prizes!"

Personal Notes:

_____

_____

_____

_____

_____

_____

_____

_____

_____

_____

_____

_____

_____

_____

_____

_____

_____

_____

_____

_____

_____

_____

_____

_____

Devotion 59

The king of Syria had laid his nefarious plan to kidnap Elisha, the man of God. And here we see that plan put into action:

2 Kings 6:14 *Therefore sent he thither horses, and chariots, and a great host: and they came by night, and compassed the city about.*

This was no small force that was sent after Elisha! They surrounded the entire city! Presently, the servant of Elisha looked out and realized what was happening:

2 Kings 6:15 *And when the servant of the man of God was risen early, and gone forth, behold, an host compassed the city both with horses and chariots. And his servant said unto him, Alas, my master! how shall we do?*

Elisha's servant had a fairly logical question that went something like this: "AGGGGHHH! WHAT ARE WE GOING TO DO?!?"

He was panicking. But Elisha was not panicking, not at all:

2 Kings 6:16 *And he answered, Fear not: for they that be with us are more than they that be with them.*

Seeing with his physical eyes, the servant of Elisha had to be a bit perplexed at this something like, "No biggie, we outnumber them to 2 to 20,000," view of Elisha. But you see, Elisha could see some things that his servant could not see, and we will get into that in the next devotion.

For now, DO always remember, each time you are about to panic, that there may well be things present that you cannot see that will change everything for the better!

Personal Notes:

_____

_____

_____

_____

_____

_____

_____

_____

_____

_____

_____

_____

_____

_____

_____

_____

_____

_____

_____

_____

_____

_____

_____

_____

_____

_____

_____

_____

Devotion 60

The servant of Elisha had been panicking. Elisha calmed him by making the odd statement, *"Fear not: for they that be with us are more than they that be with them."* And a few seconds later, that frightened servant was allowed to see what Elisha had been seeing the entire time:

2 Kings 6:17 *And Elisha prayed, and said, LORD, I pray thee, open his eyes, that he may see. And the LORD opened the eyes of the young man; and he saw: and, behold, the mountain was full of horses and chariots of fire round about Elisha.*

If I asked you what the miracle was in this passage, most people would be tempted to respond, "All of those horses and chariots of fire round about Elisha!" And anyone saying that would be very, very wrong…

Those horses and chariots of fire have been around for longer than there has been human beings. God made angels before He made man! Those horses and chariots of fire were there the entire time. They were not the miracle; God opening the eyes of the young man to see them was the miracle!

There is an entire spiritual world all around us loaded with angels and demons and spiritual creatures that would make our heads spin if we could see them. But before you get scared, remember that according to the numbers of Scripture there are literally twice as many good angels as there are bad!

Whenever you start to feel afraid over something, DO remember that all around you are the very angels of God at every single moment! God may not always use them on our behalf, but sometimes He certainly does!

Personal Notes:

_____

_____

_____

_____

_____

_____

_____

_____

_____

_____

_____

_____

_____

_____

_____

_____

_____

_____

_____

_____

_____

_____

_____

_____

_____

_____

_____

_____

_____

Devotion 61

The enemy had surrounded Elisha. Elisha could see the angels of God camped around him. His servant could now see the angels of God camped around him. The only ones who could not see them was the enemy! And because of that, in their confidence, they began to advance on Elisha. Do you remember a couple of devotions ago when we asked the question, "What part of this seemed like a good idea?" This enemy force very quickly found out just how bad of an idea it really was:

2 Kings 6:18 *And when they came down to him, Elisha prayed unto the LORD, and said, Smite this people, I pray thee, with blindness. And he smote them with blindness according to the word of Elisha.*

Here is something that should strike you as very interesting at this point. Elisha had the very angels of God, heavenly warriors camped all around him. But he did not even use them for his defense! He simply prayed, and God struck the enemy with blindness.

If Elisha was able to see with his physical eyes the heavenly warriors of God camped all around him and yet chose instead to rely on praying to the God of those angels for his defense, how serious should we be about prayer! There is power in prayer that most people never tap into, hoping instead for some "miracle" or "stroke of luck" or "random change of circumstances."

DO remember that the most powerful thing you can ever do is pray, because the One you are praying to is powerful enough to make the heavenly warriors of God seem weak by comparison!

Personal Notes:

_____

_____

_____

_____

_____

_____

_____

_____

_____

_____

_____

_____

_____

_____

_____

_____

_____

_____

_____

_____

_____

_____

_____

_____

Devotion 62

The enemy armies had been smitten with blindness. And they may have been done with Elisha, but Elisha was not done with the them.

2 Kings 6:19 *And Elisha said unto them, This is not the way, neither is this the city: follow me, and I will bring you to the man whom ye seek. But he led them to Samaria.* **20** *And it came to pass, when they were come into Samaria, that Elisha said, LORD, open the eyes of these men, that they may see. And the LORD opened their eyes, and they saw; and, behold, they were in the midst of Samaria.*

Suddenly blind, utterly helpless, and in need of someone to lead them, Elisha stepped up and led the enemies who had come against him. But he led them right to Samaria, the capital city of Israel! Mind you, he did not lie, he did bring them to the man whom they sought, Elisha, himself. But when they opened their eyes and could see again, they realized that they themselves were now the kidnapped rather than the kidnappers.

The king of Israel instantly made what he believed to be a logical assumption:

2 Kings 6:21 *And the king of Israel said unto Elisha, when he saw them, My father, shall I smite them? shall I smite them?*

That does seem to be, humanly speaking, a logical question. "The enemy has been delivered into our hands, shall we kill them all?" But Elisha gave the right answer to that question in that circumstance:

2 Kings 6:22 *And he answered, Thou shalt not smite them: wouldest thou smite those whom thou hast taken captive with thy sword and with thy bow? set bread and water before them, that they may eat and drink, and go to their master.* **23** *And he prepared great provision for them: and when they had eaten and drunk, he sent them away, and they went to their master. So the bands of Syria came no more into the land of Israel.*

The Bible makes it clear that there is a time to kill, Ecclesiastes 3:3. But there is also a time for mercy, especially when the victory has already been won. And because Israel, at Elisha's command, showed mercy and sent these men away, they never came back.

DO understand that sometimes the most powerful thing you can do is show mercy to those who do not deserve it!

Personal Notes:

_____

_____

_____

_____

_____

_____

_____

_____

_____

_____

_____

_____

Devotion 63

The last thing we read at the end of verse twenty-three was, "So the bands of Syria came no more into the land of Israel." But you need to understand that does not mean "forever," it simply means during that episode. They gave up on trying to capture Elisha. But after more than a year passed, we come to verse twenty-four.

2 Kings 6:24 *And it came to pass after this, that Benhadad king of Syria gathered all his host, and went up, and besieged Samaria.*

In case you have forgotten who Benhadad was, here is a reminder for you.

1 Kings 20:32 *So they girded sackcloth on their loins, and put ropes on their heads, and came to the king of Israel, and said, Thy servant Benhadad saith, I pray thee, let me live. And he said, Is he yet alive? he is my brother.* **33** *Now the men did diligently observe whether any thing would come from him, and did hastily catch it: and they said, Thy brother Benhadad. Then he said, Go ye, bring him. Then Benhadad came forth to him; and he caused him to come up into the chariot.*

This was the very same Benhadad whom the king of Israel had foolishly not only allowed to live but had called him "my brother." God had specifically demanded the death of that Benhadad, knowing that he would never stop trying to destroy Israel. And yet, the king of Israel had disobeyed. Now, years later, that which he did not do right the first time is coming back to haunt him.

DO always live by this simple principle: "No one has enough spare time to not do things right the first time!"

Personal Notes:

_____

_____

_____

_____

_____

_____

_____

_____

_____

_____

_____

_____

_____

_____

_____

_____

_____

_____

_____

_____

_____

_____

_____

_____

_____

_____

_____

_____

Devotion 64

In our last devotion, we saw that Benhadad, king of Syria, had come with his army and was besieging Samaria. We quickly find out just how bad things got during the siege:

2 Kings 6:25 *And there was a great famine in Samaria: and, behold, they besieged it, until an ass's head was sold for fourscore pieces of silver, and the fourth part of a cab of dove's dung for five pieces of silver.*

Under most circumstances, there are things that people would never even consider eating. The donkey's head and dove's poop would certainly fall into that category. Not only were people in Samaria eating those things, they were paying exorbitant amounts to do so – eighty pieces of silver for the donkey's head, five pieces of silver for tiny bit of dove's poop.

This was a famine of epic proportions; but it was not a famine caused by nature. This famine was caused entirely by humans. In this case, it was caused by one group of humans cutting off the supplies of another group of humans. This kind of thing happens more often than we would like to admit, but most of the time it is self-inflicted rather than inflicted by others. People make horrible choices in their lives and end up experiencing the famine as a result.

Some years ago, I ministered to a walking country music song. He had very literally lost his wife, kids, single wide trailer, pickup truck, and guitar. And every last bit of it was because of the choices he made along the way.

DO understand that while some "famines" in our life are brought upon us, MOST famines in our life are actually self-inflicted. So DO make the wise, biblical choices that will keep you from "donkey's head and poop dinners!"

Personal Notes:

_____

_____

_____

_____

_____

_____

_____

_____

_____

_____

_____

_____

_____

_____

_____

_____

_____

_____

_____

_____

_____

_____

_____

Devotion 65

As the siege continued and the famine worsened, the king went for a walk on the city wall, and a woman saw him and cried out to him for help.

2 Kings 6:26 *And as the king of Israel was passing by upon the wall, there cried a woman unto him, saying, Help, my lord, O king.* **27** *And he said, If the LORD do not help thee, whence shall I help thee? out of the barnfloor, or out of the winepress?*

The answer of the king was dripping with sarcasm. There was nothing in the barn floor or the wine press, and he was lashing out at her for asking for help under those circumstances. But then, to his (very, very small) credit, he at least asked her what was wrong. And the answer was heartbreaking:

2 Kings 6:28 *And the king said unto her, What aileth thee? And she answered, This woman said unto me, Give thy son, that we may eat him to day, and we will eat my son to morrow.* **29** *So we boiled my son, and did eat him: and I said unto her on the next day, Give thy son, that we may eat him: and she hath hid her son.*

It is almost incomprehensible to realize that people can behave in this manner no matter how desperate the circumstances may be. But an unbroken string of wicked, godless kings in Israel had produced this type of a national depravity. Mothers were now boiling and eating their own children rather than sacrificing themselves for their children. And before we look down our national noses at such barbaric behavior, we would do well to consider the words

134

"Roe v. Wade" and the 63 million plus babies that have been slaughtered in the womb in our land since 1973.

For all of the deep barbarity shown by these women, at least they were doing what they did out of desperation rather than simply out of convenience or desire not to have their sexual freedom inhibited.

DO realize that casually destroying innocent children is not the mark of a civilized society but of a barbaric one.

Personal Notes:

_____
_____
_____
_____
_____
_____
_____
_____
_____
_____
_____
_____
_____
_____
_____
_____
_____
_____
_____
_____
_____

Devotion 66

The king had asked the woman what was wrong with her. Her answer shocked even his wicked heart; she and another woman had boiled and eaten her son, and now she was upset that the other woman was not handing over her son to be boiled and eaten like she had promised to do so. When king Jehoram heard that, even he in all of his wickedness was so shocked that he could not help but react in the most emotional way:

2 Kings 6:30 *And it came to pass, when the king heard the words of the woman, that he rent his clothes; and he passed by upon the wall, and the people looked, and, behold, he had sackcloth within upon his flesh.*

What the Scripture records for us here may seem odd and obscure, but believe me when I tell you it is an incredibly crucial part of the story. Sackcloth, in the Bible, was a rough, coarse fabric that would feel much akin to wearing sandpaper next to your flesh. If you have ever picked up an old timey feed bag, that is sort of what sackcloth was like. No one ever wore sackcloth for pleasure; it was always worn as a sign of mourning and repentance.

Wonderful, right? Hallelujah for the repentant king! Um, not so much…

Notice that he was wearing that sackcloth under his regular clothing, and no one even knew it was there until he, in an emotional fit, tore his royal garments. In other words, he wanted the benefits of repentance without any of the humility that would actually mark real repentance! His heart had not changed; only his "underwear" had changed. And that is why just one verse later we find this sackcloth-wearing king threatening to murder the man of God.

DO understand that repentance, real repentance, is always marked by open humility before God and man. No one gets to continue to wear the royal robes of wickedness and still experience the blessings of the sackcloth of "repentance!"

Personal Notes:

_____

_____

_____

_____

_____

_____

_____

_____

_____

_____

_____

_____

_____

_____

_____

_____

_____

_____

_____

_____

_____

_____

Devotion 67

The king was enraged, and he was laying all of the blame on Elisha:

2 Kings 6:31 *Then he said, God do so and more also to me, if the head of Elisha the son of Shaphat shall stand on him this day.*

The king literally intended to murder the man of God that day. But why in the world was he so angry at him to begin with? Well, the most logical answer is found right here in our text, and what happened more than a year earlier:

2 Kings 6:21 *And the king of Israel said unto Elisha, when he saw them, My father, shall I smite them? shall I smite them? 22 And he answered, Thou shalt not smite them: wouldest thou smite those whom thou hast taken captive with thy sword and with thy bow? set bread and water before them, that they may eat and drink, and go to their master.*

It was Elisha that told the king not to slaughter the captured, helpless enemy forces. And now it seemed like that very enemy would repay them that kindness by wiping them out.

Be honest; wouldn't that kind of thing make you angry as well? But Elisha was exactly right in how he told the king to treat them. Furthermore, it was the wickedness of Jehoram and his father Ahab that was bringing all of these problems down on them to begin with. Either way, "killing the messenger" wasn't going to solve anything!

DO determine never to kill the messenger. When you get into the habit of killing messengers, eventually the messengers stop coming!

Personal Notes:

_____

_____

_____

_____

_____

_____

_____

_____

_____

_____

_____

_____

_____

_____

_____

_____

_____

_____

_____

_____

_____

_____

_____

_____

_____

Devotion 68

The king, in his rage toward Elisha, had sent a messenger to him with the aim of putting him to death. Elisha, though, the same Elisha who knew what the king of Syria was speaking in his secret chambers, also knew what the king of Israel had said and was planning:

2 Kings 6:32 *But Elisha sat in his house, and the elders sat with him; and the king sent a man from before him: but ere the messenger came to him, he said to the elders, See ye how this son of a murderer hath sent to take away mine head? look, when the messenger cometh, shut the door, and hold him fast at the door: is not the sound of his master's feet behind him?* **33** *And while he yet talked with them, behold, the messenger came down unto him: and he said, Behold, this evil is of the LORD; what should I wait for the LORD any longer?*

The things we see in the Bible are truly funny sometimes if we actually see them the way they were. Elisha told the men who were with him, the elders, to hold the door and not let the messenger in! Picture those men with their shoulders to the door and the messenger of the King on the outside shouting and hollering and trying to push the door open.

The king seems to have arrived nearly immediately thereafter. And it is either the messenger or the king, most likely the king, who spoke the words of the next verse:

2 Kings 6:33 *And while he yet talked with them, behold, the messenger came down unto him:*

and he said, Behold, this evil is of the LORD; what should I wait for the LORD any longer?

Elisha had spent his lifetime telling his people to "wait on the Lord." But now the king in his rage had decided that the Lord was actually the source of all of his problems, and he was not going to wait anymore upon Him.

People get like that, and they are wrong, every single time.

DO refrain from ever assigning the evil consequences of our actions to the good God who didn't want us committing those actions to begin with!

Personal Notes:

_____

_____

_____

_____

_____

_____

_____

_____

_____

_____

_____

_____

_____

_____

_____

_____

_____

Devotion 69

In response to the king's assertion that all of their problems, all of the famine being caused by the siege of Samaria, was God's fault, Elisha spoke up with the promise of God's immediate deliverance.

2 Kings 7:1 *Then Elisha said, Hear ye the word of the LORD; Thus saith the LORD, To morrow about this time shall a measure of fine flour be sold for a shekel, and two measures of barley for a shekel, in the gate of Samaria.* **2** *Then a lord on whose hand the king leaned answered the man of God, and said, Behold, if the LORD would make windows in heaven, might this thing be? And he said, Behold, thou shalt see it with thine eyes, but shalt not eat thereof.*

Some unknown man, the king's "right hand man," responded in sarcasm and disbelief to the words of Elisha. On the surface, it is almost hard to blame him. Everyone in the city was starving to death, and here was Elisha telling them that within twenty-four hours there would be more food than anyone could possibly eat. But when we are dealing with God, "on the surface" is never the right place to look; into the heavens is the right place to look. Why would anyone think that the God who can create the entire universe out of nothing in a single moment of time would have any problem whatsoever feeding a city of people within twenty-four solid hours?

DO remind yourself, in the midst of your greatest difficulties, never to sell God short; all of the things that we view as impossible are mere child's play to our omnipotent God!

Personal Notes:

_____
_____
_____
_____
_____
_____
_____
_____
_____
_____
_____
_____
_____
_____
_____
_____
_____
_____
_____
_____
_____
_____
_____
_____
_____
_____
_____

Devotion 70

Elisha had just finished making the most remarkable promise; within twenty-four hours the besieged city of Samaria would be practically swimming in food. The king's right hand man had reacted in utter disbelief. And yet God had made a promise. But the vessels through which He accomplished that promise were truly remarkable and unexpected, and we will be introduced to them and their story in the next verse.

2 Kings 7:3 *And there were four leprous men at the entering in of the gate: and they said one to another, Why sit we here until we die? 4 If we say, We will enter into the city, then the famine is in the city, and we shall die there: and if we sit still here, we die also. Now therefore come, and let us fall unto the host of the Syrians: if they save us alive, we shall live; and if they kill us, we shall but die.*

Inside the city were the besieged inhabitants of Samaria. Surrounding the city yet out of sight were the forces of Syria. But in between those two groups were four men that neither side wanted anything to do with, four lepers excluded from society, people with a contagious disease that no one would let get near them.

These men were dying of leprosy, but they were also starving to death. So they began to discuss what they could do, and the conclusion they came to was that even if someone would let them into the city, there was no food in there, and they would still die of starvation. Therefore the only logical choice was to walk over to the Syrians and see if the enemy would extend them some mercy by at least giving them some food.

In other words, these men did not have their health, but they did have their wits.

So many people are physically afflicted, hurting and unhealthy and missing the pain-free days of childhood. And when people get like that, they often feel useless. But these utterly unhealthy men would end up being used by God to save the entire city of Samaria.

DO remember that there is more to you than your body. God has provided you with a brain and a spirit that can be used to do mighty things in His service even on the days that your body simply aches to do anything!

Personal Notes:

_____

_____

_____

_____

_____

_____

_____

_____

_____

_____

_____

_____

_____

_____

Devotion 71

The four leprous men began to make their way to the camp of the Syrians. When they arrived, they found the very last thing anyone would ever have expected:

2 Kings 7:5 *And they rose up in the twilight, to go unto the camp of the Syrians: and when they were come to the uttermost part of the camp of Syria, behold, there was no man there.*

The camp was still there, and as we will shortly see all of the goods were still there, but the people had simply vanished. How in the world did that happen? The next verse gives us the answer to that question.

2 Kings 7:6 *For the Lord had made the host of the Syrians to hear a noise of chariots, and a noise of horses, even the noise of a great host: and they said one to another, Lo, the king of Israel hath hired against us the kings of the Hittites, and the kings of the Egyptians, to come upon us.* **7** *Wherefore they arose and fled in the twilight, and left their tents, and their horses, and their asses, even the camp as it was, and fled for their life.*

Simply put, God made the Syrians hear something that wasn't even there! All of them at once heard what every single one of them were utterly convinced was the sound of mighty enemy armies rushing upon them. The sound was so frightening and convincing that all of them simply ran and left everything behind; they did not even take time to mount their animals to ride away.

On the one hand, we can praise God and be amazed that something like that is child's play to Him. He can literally say, "Boo!" and have entire armies running for their lives. On the other hand, it gives us a valuable lesson for life from the opposite end of the spectrum. What I mean is this; how often do we allow ourselves to be terrified by the sound of things that aren't even there...

Worry. We "hear things with our emotions," and often those things simply never materialize. So DO make up your mind to make "let's check this out" your first reaction rather than making "AGGGGH! WE'RE ALL GONNA DIE!!!" your first reaction!

Personal Notes:

_____
_____
_____
_____
_____
_____
_____
_____
_____
_____
_____
_____
_____
_____
_____
_____
_____
_____

Devotion 72

When the four starving lepers made their way into the camp of the Syrians, they found what they needed, and so much more:

2 Kings 7:8 *And when these lepers came to the uttermost part of the camp, they went into one tent, and did eat and drink, and carried thence silver, and gold, and raiment, and went and hid it; and came again, and entered into another tent, and carried thence also, and went and hid it.*

These men had the supplies of an entire army at their disposal. Four of them. Four men. FOUR men had the supplies of an entire army...

Are you seeing the problem yet? It took them a bit, but these men actually figured it out:

2 Kings 7:9 *Then they said one to another, We do not well: this day is a day of good tidings, and we hold our peace: if we tarry till the morning light, some mischief will come upon us: now therefore come, that we may go and tell the king's household.*

God did not provide the resources of an entire army for four men; He provided the resources of an entire army for an entire city of starving people! When these four men said, "*We do not well:*" that was an understatement of epic proportions! Fortunately, they realized that and did something about it. They went and shared the good news.

Are you saved? Are you on your way to heaven? Have your sins been forgiven? The good news that you received about Christ dying for you is not just good news for you; it is good news for the world! Never "hoard" that good news for yourself; DO go and tell a starving world about the bread of life freely available to them!

Personal Notes:

_____

_____

_____

_____

_____

_____

_____

_____

_____

_____

_____

_____

_____

_____

_____

_____

_____

_____

_____

_____

_____

_____

_____

_____

_____

_____

_____

Devotion 73

When the now satisfied lepers came to the city, they shouted the good news to the porter. That set off a chain of events worth examining.

2 Kings 7:10 *So they came and called unto the porter of the city: and they told them, saying, We came to the camp of the Syrians, and, behold, there was no man there, neither voice of man, but horses tied, and asses tied, and the tents as they were.* **11** *And he called the porters; and they told it to the king's house within.* **12** *And the king arose in the night, and said unto his servants, I will now shew you what the Syrians have done to us. They know that we be hungry; therefore are they gone out of the camp to hide themselves in the field, saying, When they come out of the city, we shall catch them alive, and get into the city.*

The lepers told the porter. The porter told the other porters. The other porters went and told the king's household. The king's household told the king. And when all of that finally got to the top of the food chain, the king responded with what, under normal circumstances, would have been a logical and careful evaluation of the situation—"It's a trap; they are trying to lure us out there with food!"

But these were not normal circumstances. Elisha had just gotten done saying that within twenty-four hours the city would be filled with food!

The Bible teaches us to trust but also to be watchful. And sometimes the line between those things truthfully can seem kind of blurry. But when

God has made a promise, and you see that promise start to come to fruition, DO be willing to trust that promise!

Personal Notes:

_____

_____

_____

_____

_____

_____

_____

_____

_____

_____

_____

_____

_____

_____

_____

_____

_____

_____

_____

_____

_____

_____

_____

_____

_____

Devotion 74

The king's worry over the situation was understandable. Fortunately, he was blessed with some wise servants who knew just what to do.

2 Kings 7:13 *And one of his servants answered and said, Let some take, I pray thee, five of the horses that remain, which are left in the city, (behold, they are as all the multitude of Israel that are left in it: behold, I say, they are even as all the multitude of the Israelites that are consumed:) and let us send and see.* **14** *They took therefore two chariot horses; and the king sent after the host of the Syrians, saying, Go and see.*

Eight letters. Three single syllable words. Yet that "go and see" makes up one of the wisest, most valuable statements of principle and intention in the entire history of humanity.

Could it possibly have been a trap? Yes. But were people definitely dying each day of starvation? Yes. Could it possibly have been a cruel joke that would amount to nothing, just a bit of sick revenge from these outcast lepers? Yes. But were people definitely dying each day of starvation? Yes. Under those circumstances, what wiser course of action could there possibly be than "go and see!"

Could sinners possibly feel embarrassed if they go to church? Yes. But will they definitely die and go to hell without the Jesus that church is preaching about? Yes. Could sinners possibly feel self conscious about going down to an altar in front of

152

people? Yes. But will they definitely die and go to hell without the Jesus that they can meet there? Yes.

When you speak to a sinner about salvation, DO let them know how much sense it makes just to "go and see!"

Personal Notes:

_____

_____

_____

_____

_____

_____

_____

_____

_____

_____

_____

_____

_____

_____

_____

_____

_____

_____

_____

_____

_____

_____

_____

Devotion 75

We now come to the end of the miraculous provision of food for the besieged city of Samaria. But this drama will end as so many good dramas do, on a tragic note.

2 Kings 7:15 *And they went after them unto Jordan: and, lo, all the way was full of garments and vessels, which the Syrians had cast away in their haste. And the messengers returned, and told the king.* **16** *And the people went out, and spoiled the tents of the Syrians. So a measure of fine flour was sold for a shekel, and two measures of barley for a shekel, according to the word of the LORD.* **17** *And the king appointed the lord on whose hand he leaned to have the charge of the gate: and the people trode upon him in the gate, and he died, as the man of God had said, who spake when the king came down to him.*

When the messengers returned to the king with the word that the lepers were right, and that the Syrians had fled leaving everything behind, the king brought the good news to the people of his starving city. And then he appointed his right-hand man to make sure that there was "an orderly procession through the gate" as people went out to get that food.

Have you ever either in person or on TV seen the crowd gathering at the doors of the big box store waiting for the amazing sales on Black Friday? Picture thousands of people gathered outside waiting for the doors to open so they can rush inside to get a 90-inch flatscreen TV for $199. People will literally trample each other over something like that!

Now picture a situation like that only one hundred times worse. Picture an entire city of people who are starving to death, and then one man standing in front of them as the gates open.

Dude never stood a chance.

But truthfully, he was dead twenty-four hours earlier when he smarted off at the prophet of God, he just didn't know it. The moment Elisha pronounced his fate, he was a goner.

DO be careful what you say; it can literally mean your own life or death!

Personal Notes:

_____

_____

_____

_____

_____

_____

_____

_____

_____

_____

_____

_____

_____

_____

_____

_____

_____

_____

_____

_____

Devotion 76

In 2 Kings 4, we were introduced to the great woman of Shunem. Now we return to her story. A famine is about to hit the land, and Elisha, so very fond of her entire family, is going to warn her of that coming calamity.

2 Kings 8:1 *Then spake Elisha unto the woman, whose son he had restored to life, saying, Arise, and go thou and thine household, and sojourn wheresoever thou canst sojourn: for the LORD hath called for a famine; and it shall also come upon the land seven years. **2** And the woman arose, and did after the saying of the man of God: and she went with her household, and sojourned in the land of the Philistines seven years.*

In Elijah's day there had been a famine of three and one half years duration. Elisha, who received a double portion of his spirit, and who did exactly twice the number of miracles that he did, now prophesies a famine of twice that duration. His friend, the woman of Shunem, saved herself and her family by moving into Philistine territory for all of those seven years.

But why would she be so willing, at the drop of a hat, to pick up stakes and move everyone and everything to a foreign land? The answer to that one is very simple; she had learned through long experience that she could trust the word of Elisha, since he spoke God's words, not his own.

Everyone has opinions. But as Christians, if we expect our words to carry any weight, we should be in the habit of speaking God's words, which we now conveniently have written down for us in the sixty-six books of Scripture called the Bible.

DO memorize, study, and speak the words of Scripture. Those words are always true and speaking them rather than just spouting our feelings or opinions on the subject gives our words authority and lets sensible people know that we can be trusted!

Personal Notes:

_____

_____

_____

_____

_____

_____

_____

_____

_____

_____

_____

_____

_____

_____

_____

_____

_____

_____

_____

_____

_____

_____

Devotion 77

After seven years in Philistine territory, the famine was over, and the great woman of Shunem came back home to Israel. But while she was gone a terrible thing had happened; her lands and possessions had been taken either by the government or by some individual who had no right to them. And so, the woman used her rightful legal recourse to rectify the situation:

2 Kings 8:3 *And it came to pass at the seven years' end, that the woman returned out of the land of the Philistines: and she went forth to cry unto the king for her house and for her land.*

This is not just an Old Testament type of occurrence. Paul the apostle used his legal recourse as a citizen of Rome, appealing to Caesar to save his own life.

As believers, we have dual citizenship. We are citizens of heaven, and simultaneously, citizens of Earth. And nothing in our heavenly citizenship bars us from the benefits of earthly, national citizenship. Believers are forbidden from suing other believers over civil matters (1 Corinthians 6) and Jesus laid out scenarios in which we should, for testimony sake, acquiesce over certain material disputes (Matthew 5:40) but other than those types of cases we can and should avail ourselves of all of the benefits of our earthly, national citizenship.

DO look forward to your home in heaven, but on the way there DO take full advantage of your home on earth!

Personal Notes:

_____
_____
_____
_____
_____
_____
_____
_____
_____
_____
_____
_____
_____
_____
_____
_____
_____
_____
_____
_____
_____
_____
_____
_____
_____
_____
_____
_____

Devotion 78

I have often said that people do not find God for the exact same reason that criminals do not find the police; they are not looking for Him! If a person looks for God, he will find ample evidence for the God he is seeking. And one of my favorite evidences for God is the amazing "coincidences" that He constantly seems to generate in our lives.

The great woman of Shunem had been gone for seven years. She has come back, found her land and possessions taken and is now going to find the king so she can ask for her possessions to be returned. Now look at the timing of everything that happens in reference to that:

2 Kings 8:4 *And the king talked with Gehazi the servant of the man of God, saying, Tell me, I pray thee, all the great things that Elisha hath done. **5** And it came to pass, as he was telling the king how he had restored a dead body to life, that, behold, the woman, whose son he had restored to life, cried to the king for her house and for her land. And Gehazi said, My lord, O king, this is the woman, and this is her son, whom Elisha restored to life.*

The king "just by coincidence" was talking with Elisha's servant, Gehazi, asking him about all the great things that Elisha had done. Gehazi "just by coincidence" was telling the story of how Elisha had restored her dead son to life. At exactly that moment, "just by coincidence" that very woman showed up to speak to the king after having been gone for seven solid years.

And you surely know that none of that was actually a coincidence. The timing was improbable to the point of impossibility. She did not come that way at that exact moment by chance; she came by divine appointment.

DO watch for the unusual "coincidences" in your life that aren't actually coincidences at all, but are, in actuality, the hand of God putting all of the right pieces together at just the right time!

Personal Notes:

_____

_____

_____

_____

_____

_____

_____

_____

_____

_____

_____

_____

_____

_____

_____

_____

_____

_____

_____

_____

Devotion 79

Stunned by what he saw as an impossible to believe coincidence, the king spoke to the woman to verify that she was indeed who Gehazi said that she was:

2 Kings 8:6 *And when the king asked the woman, she told him. So the king appointed unto her a certain officer, saying, Restore all that was hers, and all the fruits of the field since the day that she left the land, even until now.*

When the king realized that the woman was who she and Gehazi said that she was, he appointed an officer to restore everything that was hers, including whatever the land had produced in the years that she had been gone. This woman trusted the word of Elisha, left Israel for a foreign land for seven years, and when she came home everything that was hers was given back to her.

She literally lost nothing by obeying and stepping out on faith.

It has been my experience that one of the main reasons people do not want to follow God and live by faith is that they believe they will experience loss because of it. Even if that were the case, the gains of following God would always far outweigh any of the losses! But this woman found that ultimately, when all accounts are settled, there is no real loss to following God's will for your life.

If you want to live a life that in the final reckoning is truly "loss free," your only logical choice is to follow God's will for your life. So DO it!

Personal Notes:

_____

_____

_____

_____

_____

_____

_____

_____

_____

_____

_____

_____

_____

_____

_____

_____

_____

_____

_____

_____

_____

_____

_____

_____

_____

_____

_____

Devotion 80

The interactions between Elisha and King Benhdad of Syria have been incredibly colorful up to this point. Elisha has healed Benhadad's chief general, Naaman. He has also been a thorn in Benhadad's side, using his gift as a prophet to warn the king of Israel each and every time Benhadad was going to attack. And then came the day that Benhadad sent a large, armed force to try and kidnap Elisha. Elisha struck them with blindness, led them into Samaria as prisoners of war, and then had them fed a lovely meal and sent home to their master.

In other words, this enemy king has seen more than enough evidence to realize that there is a real God in Israel and a real man of God in Israel. And so we find him, in his moment of trouble, forsaking his own ineffective gods and prophets, and seeking out Elisha, who is for some reason right there in Damascus at that time.

2 Kings 8:7 *And Elisha came to Damascus; and Benhadad the king of Syria was sick; and it was told him, saying, The man of God is come hither.* **8** *And the king said unto Hazael, Take a present in thine hand, and go, meet the man of God, and enquire of the LORD by him, saying, Shall I recover of this disease?*

In the next devotion we will begin to see what came of his question. But for now please focus on the fact that a man who has spent years across enemy lines from Elisha is now seeking him out for help.

Winning enemies over is not usually a quick thing. In a world where everyone thinks a pithy meme will change the world, DO understand that the likeliest way you will ever win an enemy over to the truth is by years of consistent, godly living before them!

Personal Notes:

_____

_____

_____

_____

_____

_____

_____

_____

_____

_____

_____

_____

_____

_____

_____

_____

_____

_____

_____

_____

_____

_____

_____

Devotion 81

When Benhadad needed to send a message to Elisha, he chose to do so by the hand of a trusted servant named Hazael. And at this point, you need to know that this is not the first time his name has been mentioned in Scripture. The first time his name was mentioned was when God spoke it to Elijah, who was in the cave getting over his mullygrubs, and receiving instructions on what to do next:

1 Kings 19:15 *And the LORD said unto him, Go, return on thy way to the wilderness of Damascus: and when thou comest, anoint Hazael to be king over Syria:*

For whatever reason, Elijah clearly never did this. But when Hazael came to speak to Elisha, Elisha knew what it meant:

2 Kings 8:9 *So Hazael went to meet him, and took a present with him, even of every good thing of Damascus, forty camels' burden, and came and stood before him, and said, Thy son Benhadad king of Syria hath sent me to thee, saying, Shall I recover of this disease?* **10** *And Elisha said unto him, Go, say unto him, Thou mayest certainly recover: howbeit the LORD hath shewed me that he shall surely die.* **11** *And he settled his countenance stedfastly, until he was ashamed: and the man of God wept.* **12** *And Hazael said, Why weepeth my lord? And he answered, Because I know the evil that thou wilt do unto the children of Israel: their strong holds wilt thou set on fire, and their young men wilt thou slay with the sword, and wilt dash their children, and rip up their* *women with child.* **13** *And Hazael said, But what, is thy servant a dog, that he should do this great thing? And Elisha answered, The LORD hath shewed me that thou shalt be king over Syria.*

Elisha wept because he saw the future; he knew what Hazael was going to do. And yet he obeyed anyway and said what God told him to say.

That is a perfect example for us. No matter how much it pains you, DO always do and say what God wants you to do and say!

Personal Notes:

_____

_____

_____

_____

_____

_____

_____

_____

_____

_____

_____

_____

_____

_____

_____

_____

_____

_____

_____

_____

Devotion 82

Having received word from Elisha that he was going to be the next king of Syria, Hazael determined that sooner was better than later:

2 Kings 8:14 *So he departed from Elisha, and came to his master; who said to him, What said Elisha to thee? And he answered, He told me that thou shouldest surely recover.* **15** *And it came to pass on the morrow, that he took a thick cloth, and dipped it in water, and spread it on his face, so that he died: and Hazael reigned in his stead.*

One day earlier, Hazael had reacted in shock when Elisha told him how murderous he would be. His response was, "Am I a dog?"

Apparently so.

Hazael smothered Benhaded. He smoothly murdered him, and in such a way that there would be no marks of violence, and the death would seem to be a natural result of his sickness. And then Hazael took the throne. Mind you, the fact that God prophesied it did not in the least justify Hazael's actions. But for now, I am captivated by the fact that Hazael so quickly went from being "horrified" over the suggestion that he would ever kill anyone to doing that very thing almost immediately. Apparently, he wasn't so horrified after all.

There are things in life that we rightly ought to be horrified at the thought of ever doing. But if we lose our horror of those things the moment we learn that we can "benefit" from them, we were not nearly horrified enough to begin with.

DO be horrified enough to actually not do the things you shouldn't do!

Personal Notes:

_____
_____
_____
_____
_____
_____
_____
_____
_____
_____
_____
_____
_____
_____
_____
_____
_____
_____
_____
_____
_____
_____
_____
_____
_____
_____
_____

Devotion 83

With Benhaded now dead, the scene switches back to Judah and King Jehoram. And it is not a good scene at all:

2 Kings 8:16 *And in the fifth year of Joram the son of Ahab king of Israel, Jehoshaphat being then king of Judah, Jehoram the son of Jehoshaphat king of Judah began to reign.* **17** *Thirty and two years old was he when he began to reign; and he reigned eight years in Jerusalem.* **18** *And he walked in the way of the kings of Israel, as did the house of Ahab: for the daughter of Ahab was his wife: and he did evil in the sight of the LORD.* **19** *Yet the LORD would not destroy Judah for David his servant's sake, as he promised him to give him alway a light, and to his children.*

King Jehoram was a wicked king, and the reason for that wickedness is clearly spelled out for us when verse eighteen says, "for the daughter of Ahab was his wife." This political alliance doubtless was designed to strengthen the kingdom, but instead it weakened the king! It was bad enough to warrant God destroying Judah, but verse nineteen tells us that He chose not to do so specifically because of His promise to David.

Jehoram was being given mercy because of his great great grandfather, David.

As we get older, all of us turn our thoughts more and more to our children, grand children, etc. We tend to think of things like leaving them a monetary inheritance. But there is nothing we can leave them any more valuable than the mercy of God on their lives because of how we lived our lives!

DO live your life in such a way that, even many years after you are gone, God will be inclined to show mercy to your descendants because of you!

Personal Notes:

_____
_____
_____
_____
_____
_____
_____
_____
_____
_____
_____
_____
_____
_____
_____
_____
_____
_____
_____
_____
_____
_____
_____
_____

Devotion 84

After recording the days and death of Jehoram, the text moves on to his son, King Ahaziah. And, like a broken record player, the same tune quickly begins to waft off the pages of Scripture:

2 Kings 8:25 *In the twelfth year of Joram the son of Ahab king of Israel did Ahaziah the son of Jehoram king of Judah begin to reign.* **26** *Two and twenty years old was Ahaziah when he began to reign; and he reigned one year in Jerusalem. And his mother's name was Athaliah, the daughter of Omri king of Israel.* **27** *And he walked in the way of the house of Ahab, and did evil in the sight of the LORD, as did the house of Ahab: for he was the son in law of the house of Ahab.*

Yet again, we find a king living wickedly specifically because of his marital ties to the house of Ahab! Ahab, for all of his evil, seems to have been utterly brilliant in his understanding of power and of human nature. By constantly "pulling people into his family circle," he solidified his own power and ensured that his influence would live on long after his death.

I wonder, though, why Christians do not seem to consider that very thing from a positive standpoint? By that I mean, as we are raising our own children, and as they age and we prepare to help them seek and find a mate, why do we not do all of that with an eye toward future impact?

DO raise your children in such a way that whomever they marry will be drawn nearer to God by them, and DO point them toward potential mates that will help them be drawn nearer to God!

Personal Notes:

_____
_____
_____
_____
_____
_____
_____
_____
_____
_____
_____
_____
_____
_____
_____
_____
_____
_____
_____
_____
_____
_____
_____
_____
_____
_____
_____
_____

Devotion 85

At the end of 2 Kings 8, we find Israel and Judah joined in war and wickedness. But God would not allow such a thing to go unchecked. And so as chapter nine begins we find Him using Elisha to follow up on another command that He gave to Elijah many years earlier.

2 Kings 9:1 *And Elisha the prophet called one of the children of the prophets, and said unto him, Gird up thy loins, and take this box of oil in thine hand, and go to Ramothgilead:* **2** *And when thou comest thither, look out there Jehu the son of Jehoshaphat the son of Nimshi, and go in, and make him arise up from among his brethren, and carry him to an inner chamber;* **3** *Then take the box of oil, and pour it on his head, and say, Thus saith the LORD, I have anointed thee king over Israel. Then open the door, and flee, and tarry not.*

With both the king of Israel and the king of Judah gone, it seems that Jehu was in charge in their absence. Elisha sent a young man to secretly anoint him as king, with the instructions that, as soon as he did so, he was to run for his life!

That sounds odd—but it is a reflection of a real reality that we dare not overlook. This young prophet was about to insert himself into the world of power and politics, and as such, he was likely to raise the anger of very powerful people! So he did right, and then got out of the way as quickly as possible!

This is called prudence, and sometimes it is appropriate and much needed. We may be called on to become martyrs for Christ one day, but we should surely try to live and serve just as long as we can before that becomes necessary!

DO be prudent; there is no glory in getting to heaven and hearing God say something like, "You weren't supposed to be here for twenty more years!"

Personal Notes:

_____

_____

_____

_____

_____

_____

_____

_____

_____

_____

_____

_____

_____

_____

_____

_____

_____

_____

_____

_____

_____

_____

_____

_____

_____

_____

Devotion 86

While the young prophet had Jehu in a back room anointing him, he told him the reason he had been chosen as the next king: to eradicate the house of wicked Ahab. But of all things, when Jehu came back to his men, we find that he literally thought the whole thing was a practical joke!

2 Kings 9:11 *Then Jehu came forth to the servants of his lord: and one said unto him, Is all well? wherefore came this mad fellow to thee? And he said unto them, Ye know the man, and his communication.*

Jehu thought they had put the young man up to this. But he very quickly realized that was not the case when he heard their words and saw their reactions:

2 Kings 9:12 *And they said, It is false; tell us now. And he said, Thus and thus spake he to me, saying, Thus saith the LORD, I have anointed thee king over Israel.* **13** *Then they hasted, and took every man his garment, and put it under him on the top of the stairs, and blew with trumpets, saying, Jehu is king.*

Consider this. A stranger, a guy that these men thought was literally crazy, came unexpectedly and anointed Jehu as king. Immediately upon hearing that is what he had done, the men leaped into action proclaiming him king.

In other words, they did not do so because of the prophet, the one they thought was "mad." That means that they did so because of Jehu! They had been around him enough and seen enough kingly qualities in him that they were ready at once to have him as king, though he was not of royal seed.

Do you feel obscure, unknown, unimportant? DO live your life in such a way that when God finally elevates you, those around you are instantly willing to follow!

Personal Notes:

_____

_____

_____

_____

_____

_____

_____

_____

_____

_____

_____

_____

_____

_____

_____

_____

_____

_____

_____

_____

_____

_____

_____

_____

_____

Devotion 87

King Joram, wounded in the last battle, was recuperating in Jezreel, and King Ahaziah of Judah was with him. And Jehu did not waste any time in heading that way.

2 Kings 9:16 *So Jehu rode in a chariot, and went to Jezreel; for Joram lay there. And Ahaziah king of Judah was come down to see Joram.* **17** *And there stood a watchman on the tower in Jezreel, and he spied the company of Jehu as he came, and said, I see a company. And Joram said, Take an horseman, and send to meet them, and let him say, Is it peace?* **18** *So there went one on horseback to meet him, and said, Thus saith the king, Is it peace? And Jehu said, What hast thou to do with peace? turn thee behind me. And the watchman told, saying, The messenger came to them, but he cometh not again.* **19** *Then he sent out a second on horseback, which came to them, and said, Thus saith the king, Is it peace? And Jehu answered, What hast thou to do with peace? turn thee behind me.* **20** *And the watchman told, saying, He came even unto them, and cometh not again: and the driving is like the driving of Jehu the son of Nimshi; for he driveth furiously.*

In this passage of Scripture, there are many deep theological truths we can glean. But what say we deal with a rather practical one instead.

People were able to specifically point out Jehu because of his "furious driving!"

Ouch. And yes, we are going to go there.

How many Christian testimonies have been ruined in a moment of road rage? Is that spot in traffic really worth it? Is the "single finger salute" someone gave you important enough for a mug shot?

DO remember that your testimony in traffic is every bit as important as your testimony in church!

Personal Notes:

_____

_____

_____

_____

_____

_____

_____

_____

_____

_____

_____

_____

_____

_____

_____

_____

_____

_____

_____

_____

_____

_____

_____

_____

_____

_____

Devotion 88

King Joram was in Jezreel recuperating from his wounds at the hands of the Syrians in the last battle. King Ahaziah of Judah was with him. Unbeknownst to both of them, a young prophet, at the instruction of Elisha, had anointed Joram's general, Jehu, to be the next king. He would also be the fulfillment of the prophecy of Elijah concerning the cutting off of the house of Ahab for what Ahab and Jezebel did to Naboth the Jezreelite.

And now Jehu was riding that way. He had been seen, two different messengers had been sent out to find out what was going on, neither had returned, and it was clear that something was amiss. So it was that both the king of Israel and the king of Judah rode out to meet him, and their fate.

2 Kings 9:21 *And Joram said, Make ready. And his chariot was made ready. And Joram king of Israel and Ahaziah king of Judah went out, each in his chariot, and they went out against Jehu, and met him in the portion of Naboth the Jezreelite.*

Out of all of Israel, Joram had gone to be healed in Jezreel. One tiny spot out of an entire nation. And when Joram rode out to meet Jehu, he "just so happened" to meet him in a tiny spot of that tiny spot, the property that had belonged to Naboth the Jezreelite before Jezebel murdered him and took the land for Ahab.

It was that exact spot that Elijah prophesied would be the doom of the house of Ahab. And it was.

It is impossible for that to be a coincidence; it was an exact fulfillment of an exact prophecy.

DO pay attention to things like that in Scripture, and DO realize that there is a God and He is in charge!

Personal Notes:

_____

_____

_____

_____

_____

_____

_____

_____

_____

_____

_____

_____

_____

_____

_____

_____

_____

_____

_____

_____

_____

_____

_____

_____

_____

Devotion 89

When Joram finally got within speaking distance of Jehu, he asked him, in our vernacular, "Is everything okay?" He did not like the answer that he received...

2 Kings 9:22 *And it came to pass, when Joram saw Jehu, that he said, Is it peace, Jehu? And he answered, What peace, so long as the whoredoms of thy mother Jezebel and her witchcrafts are so many?*

It is interesting to remember that, up until one day earlier, Jehu had been working for Joram! But even though his "righteous zeal" was completely opportunistic, his evaluation of the sin problem at hand was completely correct. Jezebel was still alive, still the power behind the throne, and her sins of choice that she led the land into behind her were whoredom and witchcraft.

In other words, two things that our modern society have decided are actually no big deal, or worse, even "actually kind of cool," are the two sins that God was so very angry at Jezebel and Israel over.

DO understand that God still expects total abstinence from sexual activity outside of the bonds of marriage and total abstinence from any form of witchcraft!

Personal Notes:

_____
_____
_____
_____
_____
_____
_____
_____
_____
_____
_____
_____
_____
_____
_____
_____
_____
_____
_____
_____
_____
_____
_____
_____
_____
_____
_____

Devotion 90

Some things that come out of people's mouths are almost unbelievable in their irony. Joram now realized that Jehu had come to kill him. Look at what immediately popped out of his mouth when he realized that:

2 Kings 9:23 *And Joram turned his hands, and fled, and said to Ahaziah, There is treachery, O Ahaziah.*

Treachery? Pardon me, Joram, did you actually just, out loud, complain about someone being treacherous? I seem to remember an innocent man named Naboth obeying God by refusing to sell his vineyard to Ahab. I seem to remember your mother, Jezebel, rounding up a couple of sycophantic liars to claim that they had heard him blaspheme God and the king. I seem to remember a man who had done nothing wrong being stoned to death so your daddy could have a piece of ground that did not belong to him. Treachery? Your family slaughtered a man for a piece of dirt.

That is called "not being self-aware."

It is very easy to see the faults in others; somehow it is much harder to see those very same faults in ourselves or our family. But if Joram had learned to do that very thing, he may have been able to live a full life and experience a full reign.

It is easy to be aware of the faults of others; DO make a habit of doing the much harder thing and being aware of your own faults!

Personal Notes:

_____
_____
_____
_____
_____
_____
_____
_____
_____
_____
_____
_____
_____
_____
_____
_____
_____
_____
_____
_____
_____
_____
_____
_____
_____
_____

Devotion 91

Joram (also known as Jehoram) knew that he was in trouble. He shouted a warning to Ahaziah, turned, and "burned rubber" getting out of there. Unfortunately for him, the man chasing him was way above the average guy.

2 Kings 9:24 *And Jehu drew a bow with his full strength, and smote Jehoram between his arms, and the arrow went out at his heart, and he sunk down in his chariot.*

That phrase, "with his full strength" is the perfect summary of the man Jehu. He drove "furiously." He drew the bow, "with his full strength," which resulted in the arrow piercing Joram's back and coming out the front of his chest! When he went after the house of Ahab, he slaughtered them all. This man, Jehu, who had his own "issues" before God, at least managed to avoid the one issue that tends to plague God's people even today; halfheartedness.

DO understand that we serve a God who deserves our full devotion, emotion, attention, energy, and passion!

Personal Notes:

_____
_____
_____
_____
_____
_____
_____
_____
_____
_____
_____
_____
_____
_____
_____
_____
_____
_____
_____
_____
_____
_____
_____
_____
_____
_____
_____
_____
_____

Devotion 92

God had prepared and anointed Jehu to kill one king, King Joram of Israel, and to wipe out one family, the family of Ahab. But remember that the foolish king of Judah had been hobnobbing with Ahab. And because of that, he ended up just as dead as Joram:

2 Kings 9:27 *But when Ahaziah the king of Judah saw this, he fled by the way of the garden house. And Jehu followed after him, and said, Smite him also in the chariot. And they did so at the going up to Gur, which is by Ibleam. And he fled to Megiddo, and died there.*

The account in 2 Chronicles 22 gives us the longer version of what happened here, and we will cover that when we get to it. The short version of it as seen here, though, is that Ahaziah died because of his association with evil King Joram and the house of Ahab. He could have lived a long life, but instead that life was cut short because of who he chose to hang around.

One of the wisest things parents can ever do is impress this truth upon their children from the earliest ages. The concept of "guilt by association" will always be with us whether we like it or not. That is one of the reasons that Scripture so often warns us not to be associated with sinners. As the old-timers used to so wisely put it, "Lay down with the dogs, get up with fleas!"

DO teach your children that truth!

Personal Notes:

_____

_____

_____

_____

_____

_____

_____

_____

_____

_____

_____

_____

_____

_____

_____

_____

_____

_____

_____

_____

_____

_____

_____

_____

_____

_____

_____

_____

Devotion 93

As Jehu entered Jezreel to deal with Jezebel, one of the funniest scenes in all of Scripture begins to unfold for us.

2 Kings 9:30 *And when Jehu was come to Jezreel, Jezebel heard of it; and she painted her face, and tired her head, and looked out at a window.*

Jezebel had always managed to get her way by her looks. So now she "gussies herself up" once again. She is counting on being "hot" enough to have all of the men inside rush to her defense. Since she is certain that it will work, she is not afraid to smart off at Jehu:

2 Kings 9:31 *And as Jehu entered in at the gate, she said, Had Zimri peace, who slew his master?*

The answer to her question was no. Zimri was killed seven days later after slaying Omri. But Jehu was not afraid of her threat and called out to the tower for help in dealing with her. And remember, Jezebel was not afraid of that, because she was so "desirable" to men.

2 Kings 9:32 *And he lifted up his face to the window, and said, Who is on my side? who? And there looked out to him two or three eunuchs.*

Eunuchs? Behold, the "oh, snap" moment for Jezebel...

2 Kings 9:33 *And he said, Throw her down. So they threw her down: and some of her blood was sprinkled on the wall, and on the horses: and he trode her under foot.*

DO remember that no matter what the job is, God always has some "right men" for the job!

Personal Notes:

_____
_____
_____
_____
_____
_____
_____
_____
_____
_____
_____
_____
_____
_____
_____
_____
_____
_____
_____
_____
_____
_____
_____
_____
_____

Devotion 94

Jezebel had now "fallen for Jehu" in the most literal sense of the word. The eunuchs, utterly unimpressed with her beauty, had chucked her out the window like rotten produce. For his part, Jehu went about his day as if this kind of thing were the most normal thing in the world, going inside to grab a quick bite to eat.

2 Kings 9:34 *And when he was come in, he did eat and drink, and said, Go, see now this cursed woman, and bury her: for she is a king's daughter.*

The command was simple enough. But when the servants went to do it, they found a problem:

2 Kings 9:35 *And they went to bury her: but they found no more of her than the skull, and the feet, and the palms of her hands.* **36** *Wherefore they came again, and told him. And he said, This is the word of the LORD, which he spake by his servant Elijah the Tishbite, saying, In the portion of Jezreel shall dogs eat the flesh of Jezebel:* **37** *And the carcase of Jezebel shall be as dung upon the face of the field in the portion of Jezreel; so that they shall not say, This is Jezebel.*

This was an exact fulfillment of the prophecy of 1 Kings 21:23. Once again, God proved Himself to be God in the most precise manner. And Jezebel, who had frightened everyone for decades, in the end found that neither Jehu, nor eunuchs, nor gravity, nor dogs were afraid of her.

When you see the wicked in great power for decades at a time, seemingly having no fear of anything, DO remember that their story will never, ever end with "and they lived happily ever after!"

Personal Notes:

_____
_____
_____
_____
_____
_____
_____
_____
_____
_____
_____
_____
_____
_____
_____
_____
_____
_____
_____
_____
_____
_____
_____
_____
_____
_____
_____
_____
_____

Devotion 95

Ahab was dead. Jezebel was dead. Their son Joram was dead. But Ahab had, in his lifetime, made a point to produce a great many sons, no doubt with a great many women, to ensure that his line would last forever.

2 Kings 10:1a *And Ahab had seventy sons in Samaria...*

Seventy sons. Seventy more chances for the wickedness of Ahab to live on. Little wonder, then, that God chose ultra zealous Jehu to deal with the problem.

2 Kings 10:1b *...And Jehu wrote letters, and sent to Samaria, unto the rulers of Jezreel, to the elders, and to them that brought up Ahab's children, saying,* **2** *Now as soon as this letter cometh to you, seeing your master's sons are with you, and there are with you chariots and horses, a fenced city also, and armour;* **3** *Look even out the best and meetest of your master's sons, and set him on his father's throne, and fight for your master's house.*

Jehu's manner of beginning to deal with this problem was interesting indeed. Rather than just riding in and killing the house of Ahab, he sent to Samaria and gave the people a chance to make the best remaining son of Ahab king and to fight for him and the house of Ahab. We will get to the "why" of that in the next devotion. For now just look at the response he received:

2 Kings 10:4 *But they were exceedingly afraid, and said, Behold, two kings stood not before him: how then shall we stand?*

Jehu quickly followed up his victory over Joram and Ahaziah by coming after the sons of Ahab in Samaria. And his victory was still so fresh in everyone's mind that the men of Samaria were not willing to fight against him. Jehu avoided the one thing that tends to cause people as much or more trouble than anything else: procrastination.

DO be quick to do the things that need to be done; delay in doing right is always to the enemy's benefit, never to yours!

Personal Notes:

_____

_____

_____

_____

_____

_____

_____

_____

_____

_____

_____

_____

_____

_____

_____

_____

_____

_____

Devotion 96

The authorities in Samaria knew they were in trouble. Here, then, is how the situation concerning the sons of Ahab played out.

2 Kings 10:5 *And he that was over the house, and he that was over the city, the elders also, and the bringers up of the children, sent to Jehu, saying, We are thy servants, and will do all that thou shalt bid us; we will not make any king: do thou that which is good in thine eyes.* **6** *Then he wrote a letter the second time to them, saying, If ye be mine, and if ye will hearken unto my voice, take ye the heads of the men your master's sons, and come to me to Jezreel by to morrow this time. Now the king's sons, being seventy persons, were with the great men of the city, which brought them up.* **7** *And it came to pass, when the letter came to them, that they took the king's sons, and slew seventy persons, and put their heads in baskets, and sent him them to Jezreel.* **8** *And there came a messenger, and told him, saying, They have brought the heads of the king's sons. And he said, Lay ye them in two heaps at the entering in of the gate until the morning.* **9** *And it came to pass in the morning, that he went out, and stood, and said to all the people, Ye be righteous: behold, I conspired against my master, and slew him: but who slew all these?*

We now arrive at the "why" of the last devotion. Why did Jehu not simply ride into Samaria and kill the house of Ahab?

When Jehu rode into Jezreel to deal with Jezebel, she asked him an accusatory question, "Had

Zimri peace, who slew his master?" She was accusing him of being unrighteous for daring to put someone in authority to death. But now, it was not him, but the elders of Samaria who physically put their hands on the seventy sons of Ahab and cut their heads off. Jehu was using their own standard to condemn them; he was pointing out their hypocrisy and situational ethics.

In your lifetime you will be accused of a great many things. If you are truly in the wrong, make it right. But DO be in the habit of examining the lives of those who make accusations; in so doing, you may find much more hypocrisy than holiness in what they say!

Personal Notes:

_____

_____

_____

_____

_____

_____

_____

_____

_____

_____

_____

_____

_____

_____

_____

_____

Devotion 97

Jehu completely wiped out the house of Ahab. He then made his way back to Samaria, and along the way met some people coming that direction who had not heard of all that had transpired.

2 Kings 10:12 *And he arose and departed, and came to Samaria. And as he was at the shearing house in the way,* **13** *Jehu met with the brethren of Ahaziah king of Judah, and said, Who are ye? And they answered, We are the brethren of Ahaziah; and we go down to salute the children of the king and the children of the queen.*

Just as Ahaziah, the king of Judah, had been loyal to Ahab and Jezebel, the family of Ahaziah was loyal to them as well. And that family, the stepbrothers of Ahaziah, let Jehu know that they were coming that way to "salute the children of the king and the children of the queen." The king and queen whose children they were referring to, again, were Ahab and Jezebel.

That loyalty to wickedness was about to cost them their lives.

2 Kings 10:14 *And he said, Take them alive. And they took them alive, and slew them at the pit of the shearing house, even two and forty men; neither left he any of them.*

People wanted to be in Ahab and Jezebel's orbit because of the power and prestige that inner circle brought. But power and prestige gained from allegiance to the wicked never ends well.

DO make up your mind that any power and prestige you ever have will come from faithfully and humbly serving the Lord your God and allowing Him to exalt you in due time!

Personal Notes:

_____

_____

_____

_____

_____

_____

_____

_____

_____

_____

_____

_____

_____

_____

_____

_____

_____

_____

_____

_____

_____

_____

_____

_____

_____

_____

Devotion 98

Jehu was still on his killing spree, executing God's appointed judgment on the house of Ahab. But along the way he ran into one of the most unique characters in all of Scripture. After spending days dealing with people who were promiscuous (Jezebel), sycophantic (Ahaziah and all of his family), and hypocritical (the elders of Samaria), Jehu now comes across a man known here as Jehonadab, elsewhere called Jonadab.

2 Kings 10:15 *And when he was departed thence, he lighted on Jehonadab the son of Rechab coming to meet him: and he saluted him, and said to him, Is thine heart right, as my heart is with thy heart? And Jehonadab answered, It is. If it be, give me thine hand. And he gave him his hand; and he took him up to him into the chariot.* **16** *And he said, Come with me, and see my zeal for the LORD. So they made him ride in his chariot.*

Jehu met this guy, Jehonadab, and asked him, "Is your heart right?" or, as we would put it, "Are you right with God?" Naturally he said yes. Doesn't everybody? If you ask a drunk who is shacked up with someone else's wife if he is right with God, nine times out of ten he will say yes, in spite of the obvious evidence to the contrary.

But when Jehonadab said it, it was true. So great was his righteous influence on everyone around him that more than 250 years later, Jeremiah found that his children were still living for the Lord and obeying his command to never drink alcohol!

When someone asks you, "Are you right with God," DO be able to say yes and have it actually be true!

Personal Notes:

_____
_____
_____
_____
_____
_____
_____
_____
_____
_____
_____
_____
_____
_____
_____
_____
_____
_____
_____
_____
_____
_____
_____
_____
_____
_____
_____
_____
_____

Devotion 99

Jehu had brought righteous Jehonadab up into his chariot. And now, the house of Ahab slain, the two of them together would turn their attention to wiping out the wicked Baal worship that the house of Ahab had so promoted.

2 Kings 10:18 *And Jehu gathered all the people together, and said unto them, Ahab served Baal a little; but Jehu shall serve him much.* **19** *Now therefore call unto me all the prophets of Baal, all his servants, and all his priests; let none be wanting: for I have a great sacrifice to do to Baal; whosoever shall be wanting, he shall not live. But Jehu did it in subtilty, to the intent that he might destroy the worshippers of Baal.* **20** *And Jehu said, Proclaim a solemn assembly for Baal. And they proclaimed it.* **21** *And Jehu sent through all Israel: and all the worshippers of Baal came, so that there was not a man left that came not. And they came into the house of Baal; and the house of Baal was full from one end to another.* **22** *And he said unto him that was over the vestry, Bring forth vestments for all the worshippers of Baal. And he brought them forth vestments.*

Jehu got all of the worshipers of Baal together in one place. Then he did something very interesting; he brought out specific garments for all of them to wear, garments that would mark them as worshipers of Baal. He "put them in team jerseys..."

In other words, when the slaughter started, even if any of them ran, they would be easy to identify.

People today put on all kinds of "jerseys," both literal clothing and figurative "designations of where they stand." But the thing about a jersey is that it lumps you in with the rest of the team. And if that team just so happens to be anti-God, it will not matter if you are just "a little bit on board," you will be identified with the worst of the worst who wear that jersey!

DO be careful never to get lumped in with Team Satan!

Personal Notes:

_____

_____

_____

_____

_____

_____

_____

_____

_____

_____

_____

_____

_____

_____

_____

_____

_____

_____

_____

_____

Devotion 100

Jehu's trap had been set, and all of the worshipers of Baal were adorned in their team jerseys. All of that done, it was time for the main event. And Jehu left absolutely nothing to chance.

2 Kings 10:24 *And when they went in to offer sacrifices and burnt offerings, Jehu appointed fourscore men without, and said, If any of the men whom I have brought into your hands escape, he that letteth him go, his life shall be for the life of him.* **25** *And it came to pass, as soon as he had made an end of offering the burnt offering, that Jehu said to the guard and to the captains, Go in, and slay them; let none come forth. And they smote them with the edge of the sword; and the guard and the captains cast them out, and went to the city of the house of Baal.* **26** *And they brought forth the images out of the house of Baal, and burned them.* **27** *And they brake down the image of Baal, and brake down the house of Baal, and made it a draught house unto this day.* **28** *Thus Jehu destroyed Baal out of Israel.*

This is one of the most remarkable accomplishments in all of human history and in all of the Bible. Jehu completely wiped out Baal worship in Israel for his generation. If you do not quite understand why that was such an accomplishment, please allow me to remind you that during the days of the prophet Elijah there were only 7,000 people in all the land who had not bowed the knee to Baal! Baal worship was the accepted worship for probably 99.99% of the population, and Jehu completely obliterated it. But not only did he obliterate it, he also humiliated it. Verse twenty-seven tells us that he broke down the house of Baal and made a draught house of it. A draught house is a fancy way of saying "an outhouse." Jehu put a potty right there on the spot where Baal had been so reverently worshiped.

Feel free to insert your own pun right there.

DO understand that all beliefs are not equally valid. In fact, some beliefs are so abhorent that all they deserve is to be flushed and to be flushed upon!

Personal Notes:

_____

_____

_____

_____

_____

_____

_____

_____

_____

_____

_____

_____

_____

_____

_____

_____

_____

_____

_____

_____

_____

Devotion 101

After the rousing success of Jehu in destroying Baal worship from the land, it would be nice if we could read the words, "And he lived happily ever after, the end." But that, sadly, is not what comes next.

2 Kings 10:29 *Howbeit from the sins of Jeroboam the son of Nebat, who made Israel to sin, Jehu departed not from after them, to wit, the golden calves that were in Bethel, and that were in Dan.* **30** *And the LORD said unto Jehu, Because thou hast done well in executing that which is right in mine eyes, and hast done unto the house of Ahab according to all that was in mine heart, thy children of the fourth generation shall sit on the throne of Israel.* **31** *But Jehu took no heed to walk in the law of the LORD God of Israel with all his heart: for he departed not from the sins of Jeroboam, which made Israel to sin.* **32** *In those days the LORD began to cut Israel short: and Hazael smote them in all the coasts of Israel;*

While Jehu was very zealous to obliterate the foreign false gods (Baal) of the Canaanites, he turned a fond and tolerant eye to the homemade false gods of Jeroboam, who way back in 1 Kings 12 made a couple of golden calves for Israel to worship. Jehu could have gone down as one of the greatest of Israel's kings, almost as great a figure as David himself. But instead, verse thirty-one tells us that "*Jehu took no heed to walk in the law of the LORD God of Israel with all his heart.*"

Little wonder, then, that the very next thing we read is that "*In those days the LORD began to cut Israel short.*" Jehu had started out zealous, but now his failure to go all out for God resulted in God not going all out for his people. Search the Scripture and one thing you will find is that God expects our total devotion, not simply a spot on our roster.

Not just for your sake, but for the sake of everyone you love, DO go all out, all for God, all the time!

Personal Notes:

_____

_____

_____

_____

_____

_____

_____

_____

_____

_____

_____

_____

_____

_____

_____

_____

_____

_____

_____

_____

Books in the Night Heroes Series

Cry From the Coal Mine (Vol. 1)
Free Fall (Vol. 2)
Broken Brotherhood (Vol. 3)
The Blade of Black Crow (Vol. 4)
Ghost Ship (Vol. 5)
When Serpents Rise (Vol. 6)
Moth Man (Vol. 7)
Runaway (Vol. 8)
Terror by Day (Vol. 9)
Winter Wolf (Vol. 10)

More Books by Dr. Bo Wagner

Beyond the Colored Coat
Don't Muzzle the Ox
From Footers to Finish Nails
I'm Saved! Now What???
Learning Not to Fear the Old Testament
Marriage Makers/Marriage Breakers

Daniel: Breathtaking
Esther: Five Feast and the Fingerprints of God
James: The Pen and the Plumb Line
Jonah: A Study in Greatness
Nehemiah: A Labor of Love
Romans: Salvation From A-Z
Ruth: Diamonds in the Darkness
Proverbs: Bright Lights from Dark Sayings

Devotionals

DO Drops Volume 1
DO Drops Volume 2
DO Drops Volume 3
DO Drops Volume 4
DO Drops Volume 5

Sci-Fi

Zak Blue and the Great Space Chase Series:
Falcon Wing (Vol. 1)
Enter the Maelstrom (Vol. 2 Coming Soon!)

www.ingramcontent.com/pod-product-compliance
Lightning Source LLC
Chambersburg PA
CBHW071959040426
42447CB00009B/1404